SUPERBIKE

GIORGIO NADA EDITORE

SUMMARY

4	THAT'S SUPERBIKE
14	WSBK CHAMPION
22	WSBK ROUNDS
96	2014 - THE BIKES
144	EVO CATEGORY
148	TYRES
154	WSS CHAMPIONSHIP
164	SUPERSTOCK 1000
170	SUPERSTOCK 600
174	STANDINGS
175	CHAMPIONS

Giorgio Nada Editore Srl

Editorial Coordination
Leonardo Acerbi
Created by
Claudio Porrozzi
Text
Giulio Fabbri
Gordon Ritchie (Technology)
English version
Julian Thomas
Photo Editor
Fabrizio Porrozzi
Art director
Cinzia Giuriolo
Editing
Giorgio Nada Editore
Photographs
Fabrizio Porrozzi
Massimo Oliana

"Superbike. The 2014-2015 official book"
is produced under license of the
Dorna WSBK Organization
© 2014 Dorna WSBK Organization srl

© 2014 Giorgio Nada Editore,
Vimodrone (Milano)

ALL RIGHTS RESERVED
All rights reserved. Apart from any fair dealing for the purpose of private study, research, criticism or review, no part of this publication may be reproduced, stored in a retrieval system, or transmitted, by any means, electronic, electrical, chemical, mechanical, optical photocopying, recording or otherwise, without prior written permission. All enquiries should be addressed to the publisher:

Giorgio Nada Editore
Via Claudio Treves, 15/17
I – 20090 VIMODRONE - MI
Tel. +39 02 27301126
Fax +39 02 27301454
E-mail: info@giorgionadaeditore.it
http://www.giorgionadaeditore.it

The catalogue of Giorgio Nada Editore publications is available on request at the above address.

Distributed by:
Giunti Editore Spa
via Bolognese 165
I – 50139 FIRENZE
www.giunti.it

Superbike 2013-2014. The Official Book
ISBN 978-88-7911-606-0

Stampa:
D'Auria Printing SPA – Ascoli Piceno

THAT'S SUPERBIKE

THAT'S SUPERBIKE

THE racing is always wide-open until the very end. There are always overtaking moves and upsets right down to the last curve. Titles are won at the very last round of the season. The eni FIM Superbike World Championship is pure spectacle on track. Every year predictions surrounding who will be the champion are impossible. In fact, 1999 was the last time a rider succeeded in winning two titles in a row, a sign of the competitiveness and equilibrium that reigns in the championship. The formula of the two races in each round makes the races spectacular for riders and for fans, but above all the bikes on the track are more or less the same as the ones that anyone can buy in showrooms. The spectacle of Superbike is also present in the paddock, thanks to numerous initiatives and to the Paddock Show, where it is possible for the fans to see their heroes up close and personal and celebrate their victories. World Superbike is the Championship which over the years has given bike racing a multitude of great champions like Fogarty, Edwards, Bayliss, Biaggi, Spies, Checa, Sykes and now also Guintoli. And these are just a few of the talented names that have lifted the world champion's trophy to the sky. All this is Superbike.

At every round the eni FIM Superbike World Championship attracts massive numbers of fans. One of the key features of the championship is the possibility for fans to enter the paddock and see the bikes and riders close-up. The Paddock Show is the meeting-point for fans throughout the weekend and after the races it's always packed with cheering enthusiasts.

Over the years the Paddock Show has become a true place of worship, where it's possible for fans to see their heroes close-up.

For years now Alfa Romeo have provided the Safety Car for the Superbike World Championship, and this year was no exception. The model chosen for 2014 was the 4C. At every round the sponsors also organize initiatives and events that liven up the Superbike paddock, and these are often accompanied by a massive female presence.

THAT'S
SUPERBIKE

Superpole is saturday's top event: at the end of the two official sessions, the three fastest riders are awarded.

Wsbk Championship's partners provide an essential support, in return they are garanted broad visibility on the track.

WSBK CHAMPION
SYLVAIN GUINTOLI

WSBK CHAMPION
SYLVAIN GUINTOLI

TO become world champion you need something vitally important: the power to believe. Nothing is stronger than self-belief if you want to achieve your aims, both on a sporting or personal level. In Qatar Sylvain Guintoli showed a massive dose of self-belief. In Qatar Sylvain Guintoli demonstrated that no one deserved the World Superbike title more than him.

The dream of a lifetime, a dream that came true at the age of 32. A dream pursued with consistency, modesty and sacrifice, enabling Sylvain Guintoli to become the sixteenth world champion in the history of World Superbike. It's not hard to see what his strong point is: consistency. The man from Montélimar, who has lived in the UK for years, is one of those riders who makes very few mistakes. He's reliable, and he always brings home the best possible result. His weak point? After what he did in the final round of 2014, it's difficult to say. Because before those two races, even if he had often not been able to deliver in the key moments of the season, no one can now say that Sylvain Guintoli is lacking in determination. In Qatar the Frenchman, who still has a youthful face but who is father of four children, showed that he was on a different planet. He literally dominated, scoring the first double win of his career. In the most difficult moment of his sporting life he managed to do something that he had never done before: win both races and the title of Superbike World Champion, giving Aprilia, the Manufacturers' winner for the third year on the run, its 54th world crown.

Sylvain Guintoli is a modest guy. He joined Aprilia in 2013 as replacement for Max Biaggi, the outgoing SBK champion. From the Italian he inherited his bike, his crew chief Aligi Deganello and his entire technical staff. He had a big responsibility on his shoulders, but he managed to have a good season, in which he lead the points table for a long time before finishing third despite a nasty injury. In 2014, with a difficult team-mate like Marco Melandri, he succeeded in doing even better: he won five races in one season, something he had never done before, and he stepped onto the podium 16 times in 24 races. But not only that: in the last four rounds he made up 44 points on 2013

WSBK CHAMPION
SYLVAIN GUINTOLI

champion, Tom Sykes. That's quite an impressive feat, knowing the abilities of the Kawasaki man. Sylvain Guintoli is the second rider from France to win the world title, 24 years after Raymond Roche and he managed to get the better of Britain's Tom Sykes, taking some sort of revenge for 2004 when his fellow Frenchman Regis Laconi lost the title against James Toseland in the final round of the season.

Sylvain Guintoli's career began in France, where in 2000 he won the domestic 250 GP championship. That same year he finished third in the European Championship and took part in his first world championship GP in the French round at Le Mans. In 2001 he did his first full season in the world championship, in the 250 cc class, and remained there from 2003 to 2006. In 2007 he moved into MotoGP, where he raced for two seasons, first with a Yamaha and then with a Ducati. His debut in the production-based category came in the British Superbike Championship, where he raced in 2009 on a Crescent Suzuki machine. At the end of the year he made his debut in World Superbike in the final round of the season at Portimao as a prelude to the following year with Suzuki Alstare. In his first year in the championship Guintoli showed he was consistent, scoring points in every race. His only DNF was when he was disqualified for ignoring a ride-through in race 1 at Magny-Cours, after cutting the chicane while fighting for a podium place. In 2011 he switched to the Effenbert-Liberty Racing Ducati bike, with which he scored the first podiums of his career and, in the same season, replaced the injured Loris Capirossi in MotoGP on the Pramac Racing Ducati Desmosedici GP11 in the German GP.

Guintoli's 2012 was a tough one. After starting the season with the Effenbert-Liberty Racing Team, with whom he won the first race of his career in the Netherlands, he was sacked on the eve of the Brno round for 'lack of results'. He missed two rounds and appeared again at Silverstone with a Team Pata Ducati, with which he won race 2, and then went on to do the same thing again in race 1 at Magny-Cours. These wins placed him

> *Sylvain Guintoli takes a look back. In 2014, on five occasions, no one was able to get ahead of him in the races.*

Moments of tension before the start of the final round in Qatar (below), and moments of celebration after winning the title. Sylvain Guintoli joined Aprilia in 2013, inheriting Max Biaggi's world championship winning team from 2012. With Guintoli Aprilia won its 54th world title.

WSBK CHAMPION
SYLVAIN GUINTOLI

at the centre of the rider market, and he was contacted first by Suzuki and then by Ducati for a factory team ride. But Sylvain preferred to wait for the opportunity of a lifetime, which arrived when Max Biaggi officially announced his retirement from racing, leaving the world championship winning bike seat vacant. At the end of the day, it turned out that he made the right decision, seeing as in this second year with Aprilia he won the world title. It is a title however that he will defend in 2015 in the Ten Kate Honda team alongside Supersport World Champion Michael van der Mark.

Sylvain Guintoli during the end-of-season champions' photo after the races in Qatar. Below, after his Superpole win in Sepang.

Above, Guintoli in action at Misano with the commemorative livery of the first world championship win for Aprilia at the Italian circuit in 1987. Below, at the Corkscrew, Laguna Seca where he twice finished runner-up. After the US Round, the Frenchman began his recovery against Tom Sykes.

WSBK ROUNDS

AUSTRALIA|01
PHILLIP ISLAND 23|02

ONCE again the spectacular Phillip Island circuit was the venue for the opening round of the 2014 eni FIM Superbike World Championship. The week before, the ultra-fast Australian track overlooking the ocean, world champion Tom Sykes had taken the top slot in the pre-season winter tests, but it was Frenchman Sylvain Guintoli (Aprilia), who scored the third Tissot-Superpole win of his career with a new lap record when action got underway. Guintoli, confirmed in Aprilia after an excellent 2013 season, was flanked by Davide Giugliano (Ducati), just a fraction slower, and Marco Melandri (Aprilia) in third. Both were making their debuts on the two Italian machines. Row 2 had a more British look about it, with the two Suzuki men - Eugene Laverty and rookie Alex Lowes – in fourth and fifth and Jonathan Rea (Honda) in sixth.

RACE 1
On a track where Aprilia had dominated last year, all signs pointed to a similar result this time around. Guintoli and Melandri powered away into the lead, which they held for 15 of the scheduled 22 laps, but in the final part of the race they were unable to halt an incredible charge by Eugene Laverty. The Irishman, making his debut on the Suzuki, started off slowly but then moved all the way through the field, going on to take the thirteenth win of his career. Laverty started the season the way he finished off in 2013, when he won the final race of the year at Jerez. He also took Suzuki back to the top of the podium for the first time since race 2 at Kyalami in 2010, when victory went to Britain's Leon Haslam on the GSX-R1000.
Melandri also took advantage of the Irishman's attack to pass his team-mate for second, while Guintoli finished third after leading for much of the race.

	SUPERPOLE		
	S. Guintoli	FRA-Aprilia	1'30"038
			177,725 km/h

	RACE 1		
1°	E. Laverty	(IRL-Suzuki)	33'39"440
			174,328 km/h
2°	M. Melandri	(ITA-Aprilia)	+ 2.959
3°	S. Guintoli	(FRA-Aprilia)	+ 3.034
4°	D. Giugliano	(ITA-Ducati)	+ 6.972
5°	L. Baz	(FRA-Kawasaki)	+ 11.132

	FASTEST LAP		
2°	C. Davies	(GBR-Ducati)	1'30"949
			175,945 km/h

	RACE 2		
1°	S. Guintoli	(FRA-Aprilia)	21'34"034
			173,124 km/h
2°	L. Baz	(FRA-Kawasaki)	+ 0.283
3°	T. Sykes	(GBR-Kawasaki)	+ 1.103
4°	D. Giugliano	(ITA-Ducati)	+ 2.052
5°	J. Rea	(GBR-Honda)	+ 4.951

	FASTEST LAP		
12°	S. Guintoli	(FRA-Aprilia)	1'31"421
			175,036 km/h

The Italian again proved to have a good feeling with the Australian track, which has always seen him on the podium at least once every year since he started racing in the production-based category. Fourth, but some way behind the leading trio, was Giugliano, making his debut on the factory Ducati bike. The rider from Rome ran a good race, and was even a contender for the win until the mid-point. Fifth place went to Loris Baz, who looked quick on the Kawasaki, and who got the better of Jonathan Rea (Honda) in the last few laps. Sixth place went to Tom Sykes (Kawasaki), who had crashed in Superpole, and who had started well from eighth on the grid, but he didn't have the pace of those up front. Sykes finished ahead of Chaz Davies (Ducati), who set the fastest lap but he could only finish eighth at the flag. Next up in ninth was David Salom (Kawasaki), the first-ever winner of the new EVO class.

RACE 2
Melandri started well and with just

> *Tom Sykes (1) scored results that were worse than expected, while Loris Baz (76) celebrated his second place in race 2 with a wheelie.*

AUSTRALIA | 01
PHILLIP ISLAND 23|02

Melandri (33) took a podium finish on his debut with the Aprilia, but in race 2 he made a mistake that prevented him from repeating the result.

one aim – to win – but he soon found himself in the midst of the battle for the lead with team-mate Guintoli, Baz, Rea and Laverty, who was going for the double win on his Suzuki. The Crescent Racing man, who had also won race 2 twelve months before for Aprilia, moved into the lead on lap 7 after passing Baz, while Melandri went straight on at the hairpin on the same lap and dropped to fourteenth. Meanwhile, Sykes had broken away from his group of pursuers. The world champion passed Leon Haslam (Honda), Giugliano, Rea and Davies (Ducati) to head after the leading trio made up of Laverty, Baz and Guintoli. When Sykes reached the leaders on lap 15, Laverty's Suzuki engine blew and he had to retire from second place behind Guintoli. Race Direction ordered the race to be stopped and so the win went to the Frenchman, ahead of Baz in second and Sykes in third, while Laverty, who was unable to return to the pits, saw his dream of a double win go up in smoke.

At the end of the 14-lap race, Giugliano again finished in fourth, ahead of Rea and Haslam. Seventh went to Davies, while Melandri's recovery came to an end when the red flags came out and he had to settle for eighth. In the EVO category, Salom took his second win of the day for Kwasaki with a tenth place ahead of Toni Elias (Aprilia).

SPAIN | 02
ARAGON 13 | 04

02 | SPAIN
ARAGON 13|04

Loris Baz (left) twice stepped onto the podium with second place in Spain, proving that he had made a big step forward from 2013.

AFTER a six-week break the eni FIM Superbike World Championship was back in Europe – Spain – for the second round of the season. MotorLand Aragón, close to the town of Alcañiz in the autonomous community of Aragón, saw the resurgence of Tom Sykes (Kawasaki) who took the Tissot-Superpole win for the twentieth time in his career, coming close to his own track record. The Spanish circuit, characterized by a long straight and a very curvy section, has for some time now been the test track for the Kawasaki Team, and so in qualifying they also managed to place Loris Baz on the front row. The Frenchman ended Superpole less than two-tenths off the pace of the world champion, and ahead of his fellow-countryman Sylvain Guintoli (Aprilia) in third. The second row was made up of Davide Giugliano (Ducati), Jonathan Rea (Honda) and Chaz Davies (Ducati), while Marco Melandri (Aprilia) was unable to qualify any higher than seventh.

RACE 1

Sykes rocketed away from the pole slot and immediately waved goodbye to everyone! His was a lonely race and it concluded with a dominating win, the fifteenth of his career. Behind him, his team-mate Baz also had a solitary race, finishing the 17-lapper just over four seconds behind, while the battle for third was a hard-fought affair. Giugliano, who got a good start from row 2, formed part of the leading group in the opening laps, and in the final stages tried everything to get the better of Rea. On the final lap he planned his attack on the exit to the hairpin after the long straight but crashed into the Irishman and hit the ground. Rea picked up his first podium of the year, while Giugliano remounted and managed to cross the finishing line in eighth. While the Ducati man was trying to rejoin, he was passed in succession by his team-mate Davies, who finished fourth, and then Laverty, Guintoli and Elias. The Aprilias were struggling on a track that should have been favourable for them, in particular Melandri, who after a good start dropped down the field and eventually finished in eleventh, a terrible performance from one of the title candidates.

The win in the EVO class went to Britain's Leon Camier (BMW), who finished twelfth overall in a race that saw him step in for the injured Frenchman Sylvain Barrier, the victim of a nasty car

02 | SPAIN
ARAGON 13|04

crash that would keep him out of racing for some time.

RACE 2

Sykes again powered away like a cruise missile but this time he found his teammate Baz more aggressive than in race 1. The Frenchman, in his efforts to keep up with the world champion, was taking Rea, Giugliano and Davies with him as well. The Welshman, clearly the most determined of the group, broke the record on the second lap of the race... but then crashed out shortly after! As the laps went by Melandri and Guintoli were both catching up with the leading group, then on lap 7 the Italian passed Giugliano and one lap later gobbled up Rea, before settling into Baz's slipstream. After a disappointing race 1 Melandri was now showing his claws and three laps from the end, also caught Sykes. The Aprilia man was more determined than ever to make up for race 1 and on the last lap, at the end of the long straight, he tried an attack on the world champion but overshot his braking mark. Melandri salvaged a podium by finishing third behind Baz but threw away the chance to win his first race on the Aprilia RSV4, while Sykes scored his first double win of the season, the fourth in his career.

Guintoli finished in fourth, more than five seconds off the top, ahead of Rea, Laverty and Giugliano, who had slipped down the field a bit in the final stages. In the EVO category, the first to the line was Salom, tenth overall.

The Aragón round also saw the EVO class debut of the Alstare-run Bimota, with riders Ayrton Badovini and Christian Iddon. The Rimini firm became the ninth different manufacturer taking part in Superbike, joining Aprilia, BMW, Ducati, Honda, Kawasaki, Suzuki, and MV Agusta and EBR, both new for 2014.

After his win in Australia everyone expected more from Laverty (58).

SUPERPOLE

T. Sykes	(GBR-Kawasaki)	1'56"479
		165,166 km/h

RACE 1

1°	T. Sykes	(GBR-Kawasaki)	33'38"583
			162,021 km/h
2°	L. Baz	(FRA-Kawasaki)	+ 4.275
3°	J. Rea	(GBR-Honda)	+ 8.418
4°	C. Davies	(GBR-Ducati)	+ 15.715
5°	E. Laverty	(IRL-Suzuki)	+ 19.305

FASTEST LAP

2°	T. Sykes	(GBR-Kawasaki)	1'57"664
			163,503 km/h

RACE 2

1°	T. Sykes	(GBR-Kawasaki)	33'37"223
			162,130 km/h
2°	L. Baz	(FRA-Kawasaki)	+ 0.338
3°	M. Melandri	(ITA-Aprilia)	+ 0.470
4°	S. Guintoli	(FRA-Aprilia)	+ 5.429
5°	J. Rea	(GBR-Honda)	+ 8.861

FASTEST LAP

2°	Chaz Davies	(GBR-Ducati)	1'57"982
			163,062 km/h

> *In Spain both Melandri (33) and Rea (65) took third place in the races. He was only deprived of the possibility of winning race 2 when he messed up his braking, while the Honda rider got the better of a determined Giugliano in race 1.*

03 | NETHERLANDS
ASSEN 27|04

FOR the third round of the season the eni FIM Superbike World Championship went to Assen and the 'Cathedral'. Situated in the north of the country, the track is not far away from the base of the Ten Kate team and every year their star rider Jonathan Rea (Honda) is sure to be one of the protagonists. This year at the Dutch TT circuit, the first surprise was the 21-year-old Frenchman Loris Baz (Kawasaki) who took the first Tissot-Superpole win of his career, beating Rea's record that had stood since 2010. Baz was ahead of his fellow countryman Sylvain Guintoli (Aprilia), always very fast at Assen, and world champion Tom Sykes (Kawasaki), now the new leader after his double win in Spain. Row 2 was made up of Marco Melandri (Aprilia) in fourth, local idol Rea in fifth and Davide Giugliano (Ducati) in sixth.

RACE 1

On a track where he has always gone well, Guintoli took the lead of the race right from the start. The Frenchman pushed hard in the early stages, forcing his closest rival Sykes into an error that lost him a few places. The world champion however kept his cool and began to recover place after place until he was once again close to Guintoli. On lap 17, while Sykes was sizing up his rival for an attack, the Race Direction hung out the red flags following a technical problem on the EBR of American Geoff May. Sykes' recovery thus came to an end and a well-deserved win went to Guintoli - for the second time this season. After crossing the line in third on the previous lap, Rea scored his third podium of the year, finishing ahead of poleman Baz in fourth. The race saw the retirement of two surefire protagonists, Giugliano and Laverty. The Italian crashed on lap 1 while he was in amongst the leading group, while the Irishman crashed out on lap 7 while fighting for fifth. Elias scored an excellent fifth place ahead of Melandri, who again had an under-

03 | NETHERLANDS
ASSEN 27|04

par race. The Italian, like the Spanish rider, was miles away from Guintoli, and he only managed to finish ahead of Davies, Haslam and Lowes. Tenth place overall gave the first win in the EVO category to Althea Racing's Niccolò Canepa (Ducati).

RACE 2
Assen produced Superbike's first full-wet race of the season. At the start the track surface was completely wet, a condition in which Guintoli excelled. The rain increased and forced the Race Direction to bring the red flags out. On the restart of the ten-lapper, the Frenchman didn't get such a good start but by the end of the opening lap had managed to get behind leader Rea. In his attempt to pass the northern Irishman however Guintoli made a mistake and crashed out, thus bringing an end to any chance of him taking the first double win of his career. With Rea firmly in control, the fight for the rest of the podium was heating up. First Lowes passed Sykes to move into second, then Melandri, in his efforts to keep up with Giugliano, lost control of his RSV4 and went straight on. Finally the Ducati rider managed to get the better of the world champion to score his first podium of the year, just like rookie Lowes, who was second at the chequered flag. Sykes in fourth was followed by Haslam in fifth, Melandri in sixth, Baz in seventh,

> *In the Netherlands, SBK rookie Alex Lowes (right) took his first podium with a second place in race 2.*

At Assen Tom Sykes (left) was unable to score the results he had hoped for. Below, Baz celebrates Superpole inside the Paddock Show.

Davies in eighth and Guintoli in ninth after he rejoined the race. The results at Assen strengthened Sykes' championship lead, while Niccolò Canepa (Ducati), in tenth, scored the first double win in the EVO class.

SUPERPOLE

L. Baz	FRA-Kawasaki	1'34"357
		173,291 km/h

RACE 1

1°	S. Guintoli	(FRA-Aprilia)	25'56"636
			168,067 km/h
2°	T. Sykes	(GBR-Kawasaki)	+ 1.259
3°	J. Rea	(GBR-Honda)	+ 4.116
4°	L. Baz	(FRA-Kawasaki)	+ 4.459
5°	T. Elias	(ESP-Aprilia)	+ 23.728

FASTEST LAP

3°	S. Guintoli	(FRA-Aprilia)	1'36"440
			169,548 km/h

RACE 2

1°	J. Rea	(GBR-Honda)	19'09"464
			142,251 km/h
2°	A. Lowes	(GBR-Suzuki)	+ 2.222
3°	D. Giugliano	(ITA-Ducati)	+ 4.955
4°	T. Sykes	(GBR-Kawasaki)	+ 13.089
5°	L. Haslam	(GBR-Honda)	+ 13.639

FASTEST LAP

9°	A. Lowes	(GBR-Suzuki)	1'52"975
			144,733 km/h

ITALY | 04
IMOLA 11 | 05

AT Imola, the first of the two Italian rounds of the eni FIM Superbike World Championship, all eyes were on world champion Tom Sykes (Kawasaki). In 2013 the British rider had dominated, but this time his weekend didn't start well. In Superpole he was only sixth, while Jonathan Rea (Honda) took his first Tissot-Superpole of the season, the fourth in his career. After the win at his team's home track, the Honda man was determined to join the title fight and in qualifying he was ahead of Sylvain Guintoli (Aprilia) and Davide Giugliano (Ducati). Row 2 was made up of Chaz Davies (Ducati), Marco Melandri (Aprilia) and Sykes knew that he had found a tough adversary for the win in Rea.

RACE 1
At the lights Rea was quickest away and in just a few laps had managed to open up a small advantage over the chasing group. His closest rival was Davies, but the Ten Kate rider was in superb form and even the Welshman, who usually goes well at Imola, couldn't keep up with him. In the meantime, behind the leading pair, the fight for third place was revving up. Giugliano went out almost immediately, leaving Guintoli, Sykes, Baz and Melandri to thrill the crowd. After the scheduled 19 laps Rea crossed the line all alone in first, taking his second successive win after the one in race 2 at Assen. Davies finished in second place, with world champion Sykes right behind in third and Baz fourth. The Kawasakis won the battle with the Aprilias, with Guintoli finishing sixth ahead of Melandri in sixth. The result of race 1 at Imola left everyone a bit perplexed, because the Hondas and the Ducatis, bikes that supposedly had a few problems, had proved to be very competitive in the dry, while the Kawasakis, which had dominated in 2013, were unable to repeat the same form.
Behind the two Aprilias, but much further down, were the two Suzukis of Laverty in seventh and Lowes in eighth. Elias was ninth for Red Devils Aprilia,

04 | ITALY
IMOLA 11|05

> After dominating 2013, Tom Sykes (right) was expected to score good results at Imola but instead he had two disappointing races

> Loris Baz (76) was not one of the protagonists, and neither was Sylvain Guintoli (bottom right). The Frenchman however did score a podium in race 2.

and then Haslam tenth on a Honda. Camier (BMW) was the first EVO class rider to the finish, repeating his Aragón race 1 win.

GARA 2
The second race for Rea was an exact photocopy of the first. The Irishman rocketed away from the pole slot and immediately opened up a substantial gap on his rivals. For his part Davies was unable to get the same good start as he had in race 1 and he crossed the line at the end of lap 1 in sixth place. Guintoli was the man who got closest to Rea in the second encounter. The Frenchman held on to second until lap 15, but next time around had to give way to Davies, who had put in a fantastic recovery to finish runner-up. With his victory in race 2, Rea scored the second double win of his career, his third successive triumph of the season but above all he was now in the lead of the world championship, taking over from the previous incumbents Laverty, Guintoli and Sykes. After four rounds the standings now saw Rea on top with 139 points, Sykes on 135 and Guintoli on 123.

Behind Rea and Davies, the final podium slot went to Guintoli, who won a great battle with Baz, Sykes and Giugliano in fourth, fifth and sixth. Seventh went to Elias, while Melandri could only finish eleventh after a relatively good start. In the EVO class, the first bike home was the Bimota BB3 of Ayrton Badovini.

The Italian was not classified because the Rimini manufacturer had not yet readied the 125 bikes required for homologation, and as a result world championship points. Leon Camier took the top EVO slot for BMW, replicating his race 1 win.

SUPERPOLE
	J. Rea	(GBR-Honda)	1'46"289
			167,182 km/h

RACE 1
1°	J. Rea	(GBR-Honda)	34'14"829
			164,307 km/h
2°	C. Davies	(GBR-Ducati)	+ 4.511
3°	T. Sykes	(GBR-Kawasaki)	+ 6.492
4°	L. Baz	(FRA-Kawasaki)	+ 8.434
5°	S. Guintoli	(FRA-Aprilia)	+ 9.134

FASTEST LAP
6°	J. Rea	(GBR-Honda)	1'47"532
			165,249 km/h

RACE 2
1°	J. Rea	(GBR-Honda)	34'14"255
			164,353 km/h
2°	C. Davies	(GBR-Ducati)	+ 4.095
3°	S. Guintoli	(FRA-Aprilia)	+ 5.546
4°	L. Baz	(FRA-Kawasaki)	+ 6.285
5°	T. Sykes	(GBR-Kawasaki)	+ 7.147

FASTEST LAP
2°	J. Rea	(GBR-Honda)	1'47"356
			165,520 km/h

05 | UNITED KINGDOM
DONINGTON PARK 25|05

05 | UNITED KINGDOM
DONINGTON PARK 25|05

Tom Sykes (left) scored a double win at his home circuit. Team-mate Loris Baz twice stepped onto the podium with him scoring two second places.

AT Donington Park, where the only British round of the eni FIM Superbike World Championship was held, Tom Sykes had one aim: win (and hopefully not repeat the mistakes he made at Imola). In qualifying however, the weather ruined the world champion's plans. On the East Midlands circuit, for the first time this season the Tissot-Superpole was held in the wet and it went to Italian Davide Giugliano, who with the second Superpole of his career placed his Ducati ahead of the rest of the field. Alongside him on the front row were Leon Haslam (Honda) and Marco Melandri (Aprilia). Alex Lowes (Suzuki), Sylvain Guintoli (Aprilia) and Loris Baz (Kawasaki) made up the second row while Sykes was forced to start from row 3 in seventh, ahead of points leader Jonathan Rea (Honda) in eighth.

RACE 1

Lowes took the lead at the start of race 1 for the first time in his career, but he was soon passed by an aggressive Baz, while Sykes was held up in the mid-field and crossed the line at the end of lap 1 in eleventh place. The leading group was also made up of Guintoli, Melandri and Giugliano, with the Frenchman swapping the race lead with Baz and Lowes. On lap 5 Baz decided to up the ante, passing Guintoli decisively and immediately trying to gain an advantage, while the race lost one of its protagonists when Laverty crashed out spectacularly. Baz was unable to outpace his rivals and soon found himself in a scrap with Giugliano and Lowes, while the world champion was now beginning a recovery that took him to third on lap 13. Three laps later Giugliano threw away any chance of a win when he crashed at the chicane, leaving third place to Sykes. The Brit, after passing Lowes, launched an attack on his team-mate Baz on lap 20 of 23 and moved into the lead. In the final stages the two Kawasaki men put on a terrific battle, and Sykes emerged victorious ahead of Baz and Lowes. The next three places went to Melandri, Davies and Rea, whose sixth place moved Sykes back into the lead of the championship.

SUPERPOLE		
D. Giugliano	(ITA - Ducati)	1'44"903
		138,059 km/h

RACE 1			
1°	T. Sykes	(GBR-Kawasaki)	34'23"929
			161,393 km/h
2°	L. Baz	(FRA- Kawasaki)	+ 1.538
3°	A. Lowes	(GBR-Suzuki)	+ 6.394
4°	M. Melandri	(ITA-Aprilia)	+ 11.875
5°	C. Davies	(GBR-Ducati)	+ 14.514

FASTEST LAP			
16°	T. Sykes	(GBR-Kawasaki)	1'28"779
			163,133 km/h

RACE 2			
1°	T. Sykes	(GBR-Kawasaki)	34'14"134
			162,163 km/h
2°	L. Baz	(FRA-Kawasaki)	+ 3.678
3°	S. Guintoli	(FRA-Aprilia)	+ 7.376
4°	D. Giugliano	(ITA-Ducati)	+ 10.827
5°	C. Davies	(GBR-Ducati)	+ 15.140

FASTEST LAP			
4°	A. Lowes	(GBR-Suzuki)	1'28"554
			163,548 km/h

The first EVO to the flag was again Ayrton Badovini (Bimota), but due to the regulations he had to relinquish the win to David Salom (Kawasaki).

RACE 2
After a disappointing opener, Guintoli rocketed away from the grid followed by teammate Melandri. The two Aprilia men knew that the Kawasakis at Donington Park were rather quick, so they immediately tried to gain an advantage. Only Baz was able to remain on the RSV4s' tail, while Sykes started better this time and was fifth at the end of lap 1. On lap 5 Lowes, determined to repeat his race 1 podium, tried to pass Melandri at the hairpin but overcooked it and made contact with the Italian. Both riders finished on the tarmac, leaving the road clear for Sykes to move into third. A few laps later Suzuki also lost Laverty, who crashed out on his own, while the world champion in just a few laps had caught Baz and on lap 10

> *Alex Lowes (22) scored another podium with third place in race 2. The British rider was fast but prone to mistakes.*

52

UNITED KINGDOM
DONINGTON PARK 25|05
05

Loris Baz (76) had a good race at Donington Park. Sylvain Guintoli (50) scored a good third place in race 2.

passed him, and then did the same to Guintoli shortly after. Sykes was on a different planet and he soon pulled away to score his second double win of the season, the fifth of his career. He was flanked on the podium by Baz and Guintoli, while Giugliano and Davies finished in fourth and fifth for Ducati. Rea was again sixth, losing more points to Sykes, who went away from his home race with a strong points lead. In the EVO class Badovini (Bimota) finished first for the third time and again had to relinquish the win to Salom (Kawasaki), who like Sykes scored a double victory at Donington Park.

MALAYSIA|06
SEPANG 08|06

FOR the sixth round of the season the eni FIM Superbike World Championship returned to Malaysia after a gap of twenty years, and the race was held for the first time at Sepang. The spectacular (and long) Malaysian track, situated on the outskirts of the capital Kuala Lumpur, was a new venue for many of the production-based championship riders, including world champion Tom Sykes, who had only done one test there a few years back. It wasn't new however for the Aprilia men Marco Melandri and Sylvain Guintoli, and the Frenchman took the win in the Tissot-Superpole, his second of the season and fourth in career, ahead of Tom Sykes and Davide Giugliano (Ducati). On row 2 were Toni Elias (Aprilia), Melandri and Loris Baz (Kawasaki).

RACE 1
At the start of the race Guintoli got the holeshot, but Sykes was quick off the mark as well. The big moment came at Turn 2, when Baz, trying to hold off an attack from Alex Lowes (Suzuki), crashed out, bringing down his team-mate and the Suzuki man at the same time. This was a big upset for the championship and for the mood inside the Kawasaki team, and it left the door open for the Aprilias of Guintoli and Melandri. They were unchallenged throughout and the Italian managed to get the better of the Frenchman in the end, winning his first race in Superbike with Aprilia. Guintoli took home a second place, while third went to Laverty. The Irishman, who stepped onto the podium again after a run of misfortune, did not start well but he managed to get the better of Davies and Elias, fourth and fifth at the chequered flag. Race 1 didn't go particularly well for Giugliano, who woke up on Sunday morning feeling feverish after getting onto the front row in Superpole. He was

SUPERPOLE		
S. Guintoli	(FRA-Aprilia)	2'03"002
		162,378 km/h

RACE 1			
1°	M. Melandri	(ITA-Aprilia)	33'42"359
			158,016 km/h
2°	S. Guintoli	(FRA-Aprilia)	+ 0.620
3°	E. Laverty	(IRL-Suzuki)	+ 12.865
4°	C. Davies	(GBR-Ducati)	+ 15.437
5°	T. Elias	(ESP-Aprilia)	+ 15.723

FASTEST LAP			
2°	M. Melandri	(ITA-Aprilia)	2'04"884
			159,931 km/h

RACE 2			
1°	M. Melandri	(ITA-Aprilia)	21'00"424
			158,461 km/h
2°	S. Guintoli	(FRA-Aprilia)	+ 0.166
3°	T. Sykes	(GBR-Kawasaki)	+ 2.689
4°	T. Elias	(ESP-Aprilia)	+ 5.386
5°	L. Baz	(FRA-Kawasaki)	+ 5.514

FASTEST LAP			
6°	M. Melandri	(ITA-Aprilia)	2'04"991
			159,794 km/h

unable to go any higher than eighth. Sixth and seventh went to the two Honda men Rea and Haslam, with the Irishman, who had been leading the championship after the Imola round, now seeing his title hopes fade away at every round. In the EVO class, David Salom (Kawasaki) again took the win with ninth place overall.

RACE 2

Melandri's aim at the start of race 2 was to win again and score the first double of his Superbike career. The Italian was well aware that the Aprilia was most competitive bike on the grid and that Sykes was feeling a bit worse for wear after his crash in race 1. The Italian started quite well and after three laps was third behind the Aprilias of Sylvain Guintoli and Toni Elias, but on lap 4 the MV Agusta of Claudio Corti had a technical problem and caught fire, thus forcing the Race Direction to bring out the red flags. On the restart the Italian was even more

> *Toni Elias (24) had his best weekend of the season in Malaysia, coming close to the podium in both races but finishing fifth and fourth.*

MALAYSYA
SEPANG 08|06
06

After a lengthy gap Eugene Laverty (58) was back on the podium again with third place in race 1, when Tom Sykes (1) was taken out by his team-mate.

determined after moving up one row on the grid, but he made a big mistake on the second lap and lost several positions. He didn't give up however and set off again after the race leader Guintoli, overtaking the Kawasakis of Baz and Sykes along the way for third and second. Four laps from the end of the scheduled ten, he was in Guintoli's slipstream. Melandri attacked and got the better for the second time, going on to take the first double win of his career. The podium was made up of Melandri, Guintoli and Sykes, who still had a lot of pain in his right wrist. Team-mate Baz finished fifth behind Elias, his best result of the season. Sixth went to Rea after another below-par performance, ahead of Laverty, Davies, Lowes and Giugliano in tenth.
Camier (BMW) was the winner in the EVO class, thanks to his twelfth place overall.
After Sepang, Guintoli had made up some points on Sykes, but the Brit was still in the lead, 13 points ahead of the Frenchman and 22 ahead of Rea.

07 | ITALY
MISANO 22|06

07 | ITALY
MISANO 22|06

FOLLOWING

Malaysia, the eni FIM Superbike World Championship went back to Europe for the second round on Italian soil. After a year's break, the production-based series returned to Misano World Circuit on the Adriatic Riviera. The season had now passed the mid-point and the battle for the title was heating up nicely. In the Tissot-Superpole it was Tom Sykes (Kawasaki) who set the fastest time for the second time this year and for the twenty-first time in his career. The world champion's lap beat the previous record that belonged to Troy Corser and which dated back to 2010. The Kawasaki rider was followed by Davide Giugliano (Ducati) and Sylvain Guintoli (Aprilia), while the second row was made up of Loris Baz (Kawasaki), Marco Melandri (Aprilia) and Toni Elias (Aprilia).

RACE 1

Sykes blasted away at the start and immediately saw off Elias, who had started well from row 2. He pushed hard in the early stages, and was only followed by Baz, who was however unable to keep the pace of the world champion. Sykes went on to win the race by more than five seconds from his team-mate. The battle for third was between the two Aprilias of Melandri and Sylvain Guintoli, on this occasion in the livery of the Noale firm's first world title win dating back to 1987, the Ducatis of Davide Giugliano and Chaz Davies and the private Aprilia of Toni Elias, who after a couple of mistakes lost touch with the others. The final podium slot eventually went to Melandri, who finished ahead of Davies, Guintoli and Elias. Giugliano crossed the line in eighth, behind the Honda of Jonathan Rea. Sykes and his Kawasaki totally dominated the first race at Misano, and his rivals were beginning to fear the worst.

Frenchman Sylvain Barrier returned to his rightful place on the BMW Italia

07 | ITALY
MISANO 22|06

> Two third places were all Marco Melandri (33) could muster at Misano Adriatico. Chaz Davies (bottom right) came close to the podium in race 1.

> The races didn't go as expected for Sylvain Guintoli (50). The Frenchman failed to get onto the podium and lost ground to Tom Sykes.

S1000RR EVO machine after a lengthy recovery from injury, and immediately went well; and so did rookie Riccardo Russo on the Pedercini Team's Kawasaki EVO. The winner in this category however again went to David Salom (Kawasaki), who finished eleventh overall.

RACE 2
After a disappointing run in race 1, Giugliano wanted to get away well but he jumped the start, and after pulling out a lead over Sykes, Baz, Melandri and Guintoli, he had to come into the pits for a ride-through penalty imposed by Race Direction. The world champion thus had an easy road ahead and he began to ramp up the pace, going on to take his second win of the day and his third double of the season. Sykes now had twenty wins to his name. Team-mate Baz got the better of Melandri, who tried hard to take the runner-up slot. The Aprilia man had to settle for third, but he demonstrated that he was now getting to grips with the RSV4, unlike the first half of the season. Melandri was followed home by Guintoli, Rea, who had passed Elias, and Suzuki's Laverty and Lowes in seventh and eighth. After his ride-through, Giugliano finished ninth, knowing full well that he had thrown away a great chance of fighting for the win. In the EVO class there was another win for Salom, ahead of a surprising Barrier and they came in tenth and eleventh respectively.

After seven rounds and 14 races, Sykes was firmly in control of the championship with a 39-point lead over Guintoli and 41 over Baz, who had now taken over third place from Rea.

SUPERPOLE
	T. Sykes	(GBR-Kawasaki)	1'34"883
			160,341 km/h

RACE 1
1°	T. Sykes	(GBR-Kawasaki)	33'46"932
			157,620 km/h
2°	L. Baz	(FRA-Kawasaki)	+ 5.012
3°	M. Melandri	(ITA-Aprilia)	+ 6.417
4°	C. Davies	(GBR-Ducati)	+ 7.783
5°	S. Guintoli	(FRA-Aprilia)	+ 16.248

FASTEST LAP
5°	T. Sykes	(GBR-Kawasaki)	1'35"629
			159,090 km/h

RACE 2
1°	T. Sykes	(GBR-Kawasaki)	33'55"695
			156,942 km/h
2°	L. Baz	(FRA-Kawasaki)	+ 3.083
3°	M. Melandri	(ITA-Aprilia)	+ 3.413
4°	S. Guintoli	(FRA-Aprilia)	+ 5.092
5°	J. Rea	(GBR-Honda)	+ 18.975

FASTEST LAP
2°	D. Giugliano	(ITA-Ducati)	1'36"033
			158,421 km/h

PORTUGAL 08
PORTIMÃO 06|07

PORTUGAL | 08
PORTIMÃO 06|07

TOM Sykes doesn't have very good memories of Portugal. In 2013, at the Algarve circuit of Portimão, the Kawasaki man made a big mistake om the sighting lap for race 2 and threw away an almost certain win, judging by the incredible lap record he then went on to set in the race. For this reason he started off strongly with his third Tissot-Superpole win of the season, the 22nd of his career. Behind the world champion was Jonathan Rea (Honda), back on the up after a series of disappointing races. Third quickest time went to Chaz Davies (Ducati), making up an all-British front row. Row 2 was made up of Italian Marco Melandri (Aprilia) and Frenchmen Loris Baz (Kawasaki) and Sylvain Guintoli (Aprilia). The top ten riders in this qualifying session were separated by very small margins however, and all signs pointed to a terrific battle for victory out on the track.

> *After winning race 1 the world champion Tom Sykes (1) had a below-par race in the second encounter.*

RACE 1
When the lights went off Rea rocketed into the lead followed by Melandri and Sykes. The world champion was determined to continue his positive streak and in a few laps he got rid of his two adversaries and began to lay down the pace. No one was able to keep up with him, and even though the gap in the end was only two and a half seconds, Sykes took the chequered flag first for the seventh time this season. The world champion was now beginning to scent a second successive title victory, but he was also aware that a banal error could compromise everything. While Sykes was alone in the lead, Melandri, Baz, Rea and Guintoli were all scrapping together for the final two podium places, with Davies a short distance behind. On lap 12 however, the Ducati man crashed to the ground together with Haslam, losing any chance of finishing on the podium. At the midpoint of the race the positions were pretty clear-cut, with Sykes in the lead, Guintoli second, Baz third, Melandri fourth and Rea fifth. And it was in this order that the top 5 crossed the finish line at the end, with the world champion gaining another five points in the standings on Aprilia's French rider. Meanwhile the two Suzuki men, Laverty and Lowes, managed to catch Giugliano and then engage in a great scrap with him. The winner of the battle was Lowes, who finished sixth at the

SUPERPOLE

	T. Sykes	(GBR-Kawasaki)	1'42"484
			161,305 km/h

RACE 1

1°	T. Sykes	(GBR-Kawasaki)	34'45"568
			158,529 km/h
2°	S. Guintoli	(FRA-Aprilia)	+ 2.539
3°	L. Baz	(FRA-Kawasaki)	+ 3.175
4°	M. Melandri	(ITA-Aprilia)	+ 4.042
5°	J. Rea	(GBR-Honda)	+ 7.791

FASTEST LAP

4°	T. Sykes	(GBR-Kawasaki)	1'43"167
			160,237 km/h

RACE 2

1°	J. Rea	(GBR-Honda)	34'55"154
			142,024 km/h
2°	D. Giugliano	(ITA-Ducati)	+ 6.817
3°	C. Davies	(GBR-Ducati)	+ 8.676
4°	A. Lowes	(GBR-Suzuki)	+ 9.740
5°	L. Haslam	(GBR-Honda)	+ 11.289

FASTEST LAP

18°	C. Davies	(GBR-Ducati)	1'54"118
			144,861 km/h

flag, ahead of Giugliano and Laverty. Immediately behind this group came the winner of the EVO battle between Frenchman Sylvain Barrier (BMW) and Spain's David Salom (Kawasaki), with the latter getting the better of his rival in a photo-finish.

RACE 2

The rain arrived shortly before the start of race 2 to upset the world champion's plans. Sykes tried to get a good start but had to slot in behind Rea, and he then realized that his ZX-10R did not have the pace of the Honda man's CBR1000RR. From lap 8 onwards he began to come under attack from his rivals. The first men to arrive in the pouring rain were the Aprilia duo of Melandri and Guintoli: they passed him and slotted in behind Rea, who knew his time was almost up. On lap 13 however Guintoli tried to pass Melandri at the hairpin, but crashed and took out the Italian. It was a bitter pill to swallow for the two Aprilia riders, and especially for the Frenchman, who could have

> *Davide Giugliano (34) took the runner-up slot in race 2 with his best result of the season for Ducati.*

PORTUGAL
PORTIMÃO 06|07 | 08

Guintoli (50) looked really good in race 1 but then made a big mistake in the second race. Davies (7) also got onto the podium in race 2.

capitalized on the championship leader's difficulty and make up some vital points. Now that Guintoli and Melandri were gone from the scene, Rea was alone in the lead, while Sykes was also passed by Giugliano, Lowes, Haslam and Baz. Right at the very end he was also overtaken by Guintoli, who had remounted after his crash and managed to cross the line in seventh place, just in front of the Kawasaki man. Sykes did manage to gain a few points in the standings, and he now had a 43-point lead over Guintoli, and 48 over Baz.

In the pouring rain of Portugal, Badovini was again the best of the EVO class but once again had to relinquish the victory. If the Italian manufacturer managed to build the 125 bikes by the end of August as stipulated in the regulations, then it would score championship points.

For this reason at Portimão Barrier took his first win in the EVO class with an eleventh place overall.

09 UNITED STATES
LAGUNA SECA 13|07

09 | UNITED STATES
LAGUNA SECA 13|07

FOR ithe second successive year the eni FIM Superbike World Championship returned to the spectacular Laguna Seca circuit in California and it was Tom Sykes (Kawasaki) who notched up his fourth Tissot-Superpole win of the season, the 23rd in his career. The disastrous second race in Portugal now only seemed like a distant memory and the Kawasaki man took to the track fully focused. Behind him in qualifying were his closest rival Sylvain Guintoli (Aprilia) in second and Chaz Davies (Ducati) in third, both men also lapping under the old track record, albeit half a second away from the polesitter's mark. The second row was made up of Italians Davide Giugliano (Ducati) and Marco Melandri (Aprilia), both with good memories of the US track, and Eugene Laverty (Suzuki), who was sixth in qualifying.

RACE 1

Sykes powered away the quickest at the start, followed by the Aprilias of Marco Melandri and Sylvain Guintoli, who took advantage of an error at the Corkscrew by the points leader to pass him. On lap 2 the race experienced a nasty moment with a crash by Chaz Davies (Ducati), who was fourth at that moment. After crashing to the ground the Welshman was knocked out for a moment but was able to leave the circuit on his own two feet. Meanwhile upfront the two Aprilia men were trying to pull out a lead over Sykes and Giugliano, while Rea in fifth made a mistake and went off-track losing several positions. Behind this group Elias was making up place after place, while the top 3 were putting some distance between each other. With five laps to go Melandri had a good lead on his team-mate and he was able to take the chequered flag for a comfortable victory. This was Melandri's third win of the season, and boosted his morale despite the fact that he was now out of the title race. Guintoli finished runner-up with Sykes a lonely third, while Giugliano was fourth, more than ten seconds behind Melandri. Elias finished fifth ahead of Rea, who made up a lot of places after his off-track excursion. The Irishman got the better of his team-mate Haslam in seventh, while Lowes was eighth and Baz ninth, the Frenchman in a bit of difficulty on

09 UNITED STATES
LAGUNA SECA 13|07

> *In America Guintoli (50) twice finished runner-up at Laguna Seca. Tom Sykes (bottom right) celebrates the win in race 2.*

> *Jonathan Rea (65) scored third place in the chaotic second race at Laguna Seca with his seventh podium of the season.*

the Californian track, which was totally new for him seeing has he had to miss the 2013 race due to injury. Baz finished ahead of his fellow Kawasaki rider Salom (Kawasaki), who again won the EVO class. Laguna Seca also saw the debut of Leon Camier on the MV Agusta as replacement for Claudio Corti, injured in Portugal.

RACE 2

The second encounter at Laguna Seca turned out to be a bit of a crazy affair. As in 2013 the race was stopped twice. The first due to a crash, luckily without any consequences, for the British rider Alex Lowes (Suzuki) at the Corkscrew, then because of one involving Frenchman Sylvain Barrier (BMW), who crashed against the pit-wall, losing his senses for a few moments. Luckily, again, there were no serious consequences so the Race Direction decided to restart the race over a distance of just seven laps. On the third and final restart Melandri powered away well but at the end of lap 1 he crashed, thus wasting a chance of scoring a double win. Sykes took the lead of the race, followed by Guintoli and Giugliano. The Italian then crashed at the Corkscrew on lap 3, while Sykes went on to win his eighth race of the year, and the 22nd in his career. The runner-up slot went to Guintoli, whose points gap to Sykes was getting wider all the time. After Laguna Seca, in fact, the Frenchman was 44 points down on Sykes while Rea, third at the flag, was once again third in the championship but 64 points down on the leader. Fourth place in race 2 went to Laverty, ahead of Elias and Baz. Salom finished seventh to notch up another EVO win, ahead of Alessandro Andreozzi (Kawasaki) in ninth, the best result in his career in the production-based racing series.

SUPERPOLE

	T. Sykes	(GBR-Kawasaki)	1'21"811
			158,854 km/h

RACE 1

1°	M. Melandri	(ITA-Aprilia)	35'07"782
			154,143 km/h
2°	S. Guintoli	(FRA-Aprilia)	+ 0.905
3°	T. Sykes	(GBR-Kawasaki)	+ 6.627
4°	D. Giugliano	(ITA-Ducati)	+ 13.574
5°	T. Elias	(ESP-Aprilia)	+ 13.855

FASTEST LAP

7°	S. Guintoli	(FRA-Aprilia)	1'23"559
			155,531 km/h

RACE 2

1°	T. Sykes	(GBR-Kawasaki)	9'51"346
			153,839 km/h
2°	S. Guintoli	(FRA-Aprilia)	+ 1.014
3°	J. Rea	(GBR-Honda)	+ 2.793
4°	E. Laverty	(IRL-Suzuki)	+ 3.681
5°	T. Elias	(ESP-Aprilia)	+ 4.165

FASTEST LAP

2°	D. Giugliano	(ITA-Ducati)	1'23"403
			155,822 km/h

SPAIN
JEREZ 07|09

SPAIN|10
JEREZ 07|09

AFTER the long summer break, the eni FIM Superbike World Championship was back in action for the tenth round of the season. The legendary Jerez circuit in Andalusia, located about 100 km south of Seville, was in the calendar for the second year in a row and it had already been the venue for numerous winter testing sessions. All eyes were on the world champion Tom Sykes (Kawasaki), quick there all winter, but the Tissot-Superpole win went instead to his team-mate Loris Baz, who set the new circuit record and would start from the top grid slot for the second time this season and in his career. Alongside him on the front row was Davide Giugliano (Ducati) in second and Tom Sykes in third. They were followed by the Aprilia men, Marco Melandri and Sylvain Guintoli, fourth and fifth, and Eugene Laverty (Suzuki) in sixth.

RACE 1
At the start of the race, Guintoli was quick off the mark from row 2 and immediately took the lead, followed by a determined Alex Lowes (Suzuki) and by Baz. Melandri, Sykes and Giugliano all failed to get a good start, but the Ducati rider soon began a recovery that in five laps saw him move from seventh to third. Meanwhile Baz took over at the front from Guintoli, while Melandri and Sykes seemed to be excluded from the battle for the win. The two men at the front swapped places numerous times, Melandri slowly began to make up positions while Sykes was unable to move up any higher than seventh. On lap 12 Giugliano, in an effort to keep up with Melandri, crashed out to put paid to his dreams of glory, while the Aprilia man now had Baz in his sights for second place. On lap 14 Melandri tried to attack the Frenchman who in his attempts to resist, lost the front and finished on the tarmac. With Melandri in such good

SUPERPOLE		
L. Baz	(FRA-Kawasaki)	1'40"298
		158,755 km/h

RACE 1			
1°	M. Melandri	(ITA-Aprilia)	34'20"164
			154,578 km/h
2°	S. Guintoli	(FRA-Aprilia)	+ 1.397
3°	C. Davies	(GBR-Ducati)	+ 4.283
4°	J. Rea	(GBR-Honda)	+ 5.705
5°	T. Sykes	(GBR-Kawasaki)	+ 6.979

FASTEST LAP			
2°	D. Giugliano	(ITA-Ducati)	1'41"939
			156,199 km/h

RACE 2			
1°	M. Melandri	(ITA-Aprilia)	34'25"940
			154,146 km/h
2°	S. Guintoli	(FRA-Aprilia)	+ 2.845
3°	T. Sykes	(GBR-Kawasaki)	+ 6.097
4°	C. Davies	(GBR-Ducati)	+ 7.749
5°	J. Rea	(GBR-Honda)	+ 7.935

FASTEST LAP			
3°	S. Guintoli	(FRA-Aprilia)	1'42"223
			155,765 km/h

form, Guintoli was on borrowed time at the front and in fact, on lap 17 of the scheduled twenty, the Italian passed his team-mate who could not respond. Melandri went on to win his fifth race of the season, while Guintoli had to settle for a second place that did however allow him to make up some points on Sykes, who was only fifth at the chequered flag. The podium was completed by Chaz Davies (Ducati), third after a good race, while Jonathan Rea (Honda) was fourth to finish.

David Salom (Kawasaki) in ninth, was the first rider to finish in the EVO category, which now had to do without the Bimotas of Ayrton Badovini and Christian Iddon, now excluded from the world championship because the Rimini firm still had not readied the 125 bikes required by the rules.

RACE 2
At the start of race 2 Melandri's aim was to not repeat the error he made at Laguna Seca and score a double win.

> Jonathan Rea (65) produced two superb races at Jerez while Sykes (1) was a bit disappointing, even though he did take a podium in race 2.

SPAIN 10
JEREZ 07|09

With third place in race 1, Chaz Davies (7) scored his fourth podium of the year. The Welshman then finished race 2 in fourth.

The Italian was not quick off the mark however and at the end of lap 1 was only fifth, while ahead of everyone was Baz, followed by Giugliano, Guintoli and Sykes. Melandri began to make up ground and was soon in third place, while Baz started to lose positions and was no longer involved in the fight for the win. While Guintoli was leading Sykes, Melandri in third was getting closer and closer all the time. On lap 11 he was second and on lap 16 he took the lead, going on to win race 2 for his second double win of the season. Guintoli again finished second, thus gaining further points on Sykes in third, who left Jerez with 31 points lead over the Frenchman, with two rounds (four races) remaining until the end of the season.

Jerez was not a particularly good event for Giugliano. After crashing out of race 1, the Italian was forced to retire from the second encounter. It was another blow for Giugliano, who after going well again in qualifying, was once again unable to bring home a good race result. Jerez did bring more joy however for Davies and Rea, who were fourth and fifth at the chequered flag after positive races for both of them.

In the EVO category, this time it was Salom's turn to miss out on the win, which went to Sylvain Barrier (BMW), eleventh overall and back to full fitness again after his nasty crash at Laguna Seca.

11 FRANCE
MAGNY-COURS 05|10

11 | FRANCE
MAGNY-COURS 05|10

FOR the eleventh round of the season the eni FIM Superbike World Championship touched base in the heart of France, at Magny-Cours. On the home track for Sylvain Guintoli (Aprilia), the world champion Tom Sykes (Kawasaki) went on the attack, taking a Tissot-Superpole win together with a new track record, and finishing ahead of Davide Giugliano (Ducati) and Jonathan Rea (Honda). Guintoli qualified fourth, on row 2, ahead of his team-mate Marco Melandri (Aprilia) and Loris Baz (Kawasaki). With the weather forecast looking uncertain, the 2014 Superbike title contenders knew that they had to have maximum support from their team-mates, because with just four races remaining (two in France and the final two in Qatar), the battle for the production-based title was still wide-open.

RACE 1

As predicted, Sunday morning at the Magny-Cours track brought with it the rain. It began to fall after two days of practice in the dry and threw things completely wide-open. These were ideal conditions for Guintoli, who took control at the front on lap 2 from Rea, with Sykes in third. Davies also got a good start but the Welshman was victim of a crash under braking for the hairpin, while Melandri and Baz were some way behind. Guintoli and Rea looked perfectly at ease on the wet surface of the French track, but the same could not be said of the world champion. Sykes made a mistake in trying to keep up with Giugliano (Ducati), who then crashed, and was passed by Melandri and Baz, which did its best to unnerve the Aprilia and Kawasaki boxes. Melandri was in great form, and on lap 14 he passed Guintoli and pulled out a lead, while Baz in third did the same to Sykes. With the title at stake, every point was precious, so first the Aprilia team and then Kawasaki signalled to Melandri and Baz to yield their positions respectively to Guintoli and Sykes. And the two riders obeyed: on lap 17 Melandri slowed and let Guintoli through into first, while Baz, fourth behind Rea, gave up his position to Sykes on the final lap. The rain caused problems for quite a few riders, in addition to the world

11 | FRANCE
MAGNY-COURS 05 | 10

champion. There were a lot of crashes in race 1, but this did not detract from the performance of wild-card Lorenzo Lanzi (Ducati), who was eighth at the flag. The first EVO rider home was Sylvain Barrier (BMW) in tenth, ahead of Niccolò Canepa (Ducati), eleventh and second EVO at the finish.

RACE 2
After the win in race 1, which allowed Guintoli to reduce the gap to Sykes from 31 to 19 points, the Frenchman had only one aim in race 2 and that was to win again. The only problem was that he didn't get off to such a good start. Giugliano powered away ahead of the field, but he then crashed on lap 3, betrayed by the wet surface.

The lead passed to Rea, followed by Melandri, Guintoli and Sykes. The Frenchman was on top form, taking the lead of the race on lap 11 when Rea crashed at the same corner that had betrayed the Ducati man, but he didn't take account of his team-mate Melandri, who passed him on the following lap and moved into the lead. Despite numerous indications from the pit-wall, Melandri refused to give up his position to Guintoli and went on to win his sixth race of the season, the nineteenth in his career.

Behind the two Aprilias, Sykes had his work cut out to hold off Haslam (Honda), who passed him with three laps to go and edge him out of the final podium place. For the British

> *Jonathan Rea stepped onto the podium with a third place in race 1 at Magny-Cours. The Honda man was extremely quick in the wet in France.*

Leon Haslam hadn't been on the podium since 2010. In France, he scored a third place in race 2. Below, Tom Sykes being awarded the Superpole prize by Ruben Xaus.

rider it was the first podium of the year, a result he had not achieved since 2012. Sykes, on the other hand lost more points to Guintoli, and the gap between them was now down to 12. With 50 points still up for grabs in the final races in Qatar, things were a bit too close for comfort.

After his great result in race 1, Lanzi scored an incredible fifth in race 2. It was a superb achievement for the Italian, wild-card rider in France, and he finished ahead of his team-mate Max Neukirchner and Baz, while Claudio Corti on the MV Agusta scored his best result of the year with an eighth place.

In the EVO class, the first rider to the finish was Niccolò Canepa, tenth overall with a Ducati.

SUPERPOLE

T. Sykes	(GBR-Kawasaki)	1'36"366
		138,818 km/h

RACE 1

1°	S. Guintoli	(FRA-Aprilia)	36'45"206
			160,189 km/h
2°	M. Melandri	(ITA-Aprilia)	+ 2.257
3°	J. Rea	(GBR-Honda)	+ 5.954
4°	T. Sykes	(GBR-Kawasaki)	+ 15.670
5°	L. Baz	(FRA-Kawasaki)	+ 16.149

FASTEST LAP

11°	M. Melandri	(ITA-Aprilia)	1'54"013
			139,279 km/h

RACE 2

1°	M. Melandri	(ITA-Aprilia)	36'25"402
			138,058 km/h
2°	S. Guintoli	(FRA-Aprilia)	+ 2.669
3°	L. Haslam	(GBR-Honda)	+ 16.450
4°	T. Sykes	(GBR-Kawasaki)	+ 20.759
5°	L. Lanzi	(ITA-Ducati)	+ 46.689

FASTEST LAP

10°	S. Guintoli	(FRA-Aprilia)	1'53"660
			139,711 km/h

QATAR | 12
LOSAIL 02|11

FOR the final round of the season, the eni FIM Superbike World Championship returned to Qatar, where it hadn't been since 2009. For the first time however, the production-based bikes practiced and raced in the evening, illuminated by the incredible spotlights of the Arabian Peninsula track. The final Tissot-Superpole of the year surprisingly went to Davide Giugliano, who with his Ducati took two seconds off Spies' record to set his third pole in 2014. He was accompanied on the front row by Kawasaki men, Loris Baz and Tom Sykes in second and third. Row 2 was made up of Chaz Davies on the second factory Ducati, ahead of Sylvain Guintoli, only fifth despite a very quick Aprilia, while Leon Haslam, sixth for Honda, was also well on the pace. Marco Melandri could only manage eighth and he lined up on row 3, wedged in between the Honda of Jonathan Rea in seventh and Eugene Laverty, ninth with the Suzuki.

RACE 1
The moments before the start were full of tension. In two races Sykes and Guintoli would be playing out the 2014 world championship. Sykes had to defend his 12 points lead, Guintoli had to attack and before the race he made his intentions clear: he was there to win both races. When the lights went off, Sykes rocketed away into the lead, followed by Rea, Baz and Guintoli. The world champion only remained in that position for one lap however because at the start of lap 2 he had already been demoted to third behind Baz and Rea, with Guintoli right behind. Aprilia's French rider was unstoppable. He showed a steely determination and with the aid of a bike that was extraordinarily quick on the straight, in 12 laps he had already taken over upfront and pulled out a good lead. For Sykes in third, the only hope was that his teammate Baz would give up his position. The Frenchman though, despite the signals coming from the pit-wall, crossed the line in second place behind Guintoli, who took a well-deserved fourth win of the season. Sykes, third and very disappointed, now only had a three-point lead over his Aprilia rival. Losail, with its fast corners, was not the most suitable track for his riding style and his Kawasaki was unable to do anything about the Aprilia on the long straight. The only thing he could do was to finish ahead of Guintoli, but in these conditions there was very little hope of that, especially because Rea, fourth at the chequered flag, was on top form

> Above, in Qatar Jonathan Rea from Northern Ireland gave two very good performances. Below, Tom Sykes honourably lost the title fight with Guintoli. Marco Melandri (33) had two below-par races in Qatar.

QATAR | 12
LOSAIL 02|11

in Qatar. Even Giugliano and Elias, fifth and sixth respectively, could have their say in the outcome, as well as Melandri, who was only eighth in race 1 but ready for the rematch in the second race.

As for the EVO class, in race 1 the first to the finish was Niccolò Canepa (Ducati), twelfth overall.

RACE 2

Tom Sykes also got a good start in the final race of 2014. At the end of lap 1 he was in the lead but then had to make way for Rea, who was riding so well in the final race of his career for Honda. Both Brits however were unable to do anything about the incredible Frenchman Guintoli, who took over up front on lap 5 riding in a way that he had rarely shown in SBK. The Aprilia man desperately wanted the title, and for the first time in his career saw before him a real possibility of becoming world champion, so he was determined not to fail. Behind, Sykes's hopes of fighting for his second successive title were becoming slimmer by the minute. Determination soon turned to disappointment and in the final stages he even lost the runner-up slot to Jonathan Rea. At the end of the scheduled 17 laps Guintoli was first, thus becoming the 2014 Superbike World Champion. Rea was second and Sykes, in third, had to settle for the runner-up slot in the championship. Race 2 saw the return of Melandri, who was fourth after a below-par first encounter. The Italian finished ahead of Davies, Elias and Baz. After a good race 1 the Kawasaki man was forced wide at the first corner and lost several positions. On lap 1 he was sixteenth, but he managed to recover to seventh.

Giugliano, on the other hand, was unable to be as incisive as he had been in the first race and could only finish eighth at the flag, despite a good start.

Amongst the EVO riders, the first to cross the line was Kawasaki's David Salom, who was eleventh overall and the first name to go down in the record books in this new category in the production-based world championship.

> *Loris Baz was very quick in race 1 but he was surrounded by controversy for not obeying team orders.*

SUPERPOLE

	D. Giugliano	(ITA-Ducati)	1'57"033
			165,492 km/h

RACE 1

1°	S. Guintoli	(FRA-Aprilia)	33'46.738
			162,456 km/h
2°	L. Baz	(FRA-Kawasaki)	+ 2.650
3°	T. Sykes	(GBR-Kawasaki)	+ 3.955
4°	J. Rea	(GBR-Honda)	+ 4.805
5°	D. Giugliano	(ITA-Ducati)	+ 7.861

FASTEST LAP

2°	L. Baz	(FRA-Kawasaki)	1'58.096
			164,002 km/h

RACE 2

1°	S. Guintoli	(FRA-Aprilia)	33'41.803
			162,853 km/h
2°	J. Rea	(GBR-Honda)	+ 3.568
3°	T. Sykes	(GBR-Kawasaki)	+ 5.092
4°	M. Melandri	(ITA-Aprilia)	+ 8.305
5°	C. Davies	(GBR-Ducati)	+ 8.390

FASTEST LAP

8°	S. Guintoli	(FRA-Aprilia)	1'57.906
			164,266 km/h

THE BIKES | 2014
NINE LIVES

THE entry list in terms of manufacturers in 2014 was simply vast, with eight homologated manufacturers running individual motorcycle models, and if you also include Evo entries on a regular basis, the technical diversity inside the SBK class was inflated to an even greater record level.

From all new entries like Hero EBR and MV Agusta to the ever-present Ducati, Kawasaki and Honda, variety was the spice of racing life.

Full 1000cc straight fours from BMW, Honda, Kawasaki, Suzuki and MV Agusta clashed with the vee four Aprilia, and not one but two full 1200cc vee twins, from Ducati and Hero EBR.

Never had such diversity met with such determination to succeed in a year when lots of technical rule changes and restrictions arrived in the WSBK paddock; changes that were to be the vanguard of far greater ones in 2015.

From the ageing or simpler machines to the most modern or radical, WSBK once more offered plenty of scope for different manufactures to compete on a playing field that has never been more accessible.

RULES CHANGES

A true reformatting of the SBK class in 2014 saw limits brought in for many components key to final success, with every main specialist racing chassis part – brake and suspension – limited in price and available to all. This was the beginning of a road that would become an Autostrada in 2015, with electronics and many other costs limited.

Even in 2014 the effects were immediate and universal. Eight engines per rider per season in SBK, and six per rider in the Evo class, were the new limits on use, all designed to reduce costs through the year.

The minimum weight of 165kg applied for all, with the potential for the twin cylinder machines to be made heavier or lighter, and then feature air-intake

restrictors, under the performance balancing rules. Any new vee-twin (the EBR, for example) was exempt from this rule for two years.

Tyres were limited to 24 per rider in each event, 10 fronts and 24 rears, with those moving from Superpole 1 to Superpole 2 getting one more qualifying tyre as they had one more track session than any other riders. Only 13 of the allocated tyres were allowed to be mounted on wheel rims at any time.

Gearboxes were also limited in 2014, with either three gearbox ratio options, or two gearbox ratio options with two primary drive change options. Again, this was to reduce costs.

EVO MACHINES

The Evo class differed in many ways from the full SBK class and as a popularity contest it was a winner first time out. More than ten bikes were at each round, even if not all manufacturers felt that could field a competitive Evo machine.

In reality, Kawasaki was the Evo bike of choice, with entries from team Pedercini, Iron Brain Grillini, MRS, Mahi Racing Team India and – last but usually first – the official Kawasaki Racing Team.

Ducati and Althea Racing had the lone Evo Ducati 1199 R Panigale and it was competitive in most early races.

BMW's were rare but fast for the Motorrad Italia team, and slightly less so for the lone Team Toth entry.

Only three manufacturers' machines made up the entire Evo Entry, but the Evo grid was still very healthy in numbers and good teams.

'Evos' had to use a Superstock level electronics and throttle body package, with one alternate ECU system, and no internal engine modifications were allowed. They could use close-ratio racing gearboxes, but only one set of ratios, determined at the start of the season. Other gearing changes could be made by changing sprockets. Superstock level engines, only six per rider per season, were the most obvious departure from the full SBK norm.

On the chassis side, the links to Superbike were much closer, but still subject to the same brake and suspension limits. In essence, the entire class can be considered to be Superstock in engine spec, Superbike in chassis spec.

In the Evo class for a time was the Bimota BB3, run by Alstare Bimota, but not scoring points until the first homologation numbers were met. As the factory could not make the required 125 bikes by the end of August deadline, the team went from not scoring points to not being able to race at all until the second homologation levels was reached in the winter months.

APRILIA
RSV4 FACTORY

FULL COMPETITION MODE

THE old warhorse has found itself gradually laden with more and more limits to its race-oriented design but the stopwatches were still impressed by its racetrack performance. It was a championship contender all the way in 2014.

As engine configurations go, probably the most suited to racing is the vee-four of the Aprilia, with its funky firing intervals, ideal mass centralisation and high-revving nature compared to a twin.

Is it the best of all worlds? Well, since the advent of electronics has helped the inline 'screamer' fours mimic twins in most other regards, the Aprilia has had an increasingly hard time of it, but it is still the best starting platform.

When strict engine limits of eight per rider per season came in this year many prophesied the end of the Aprilia as the fastest in pure top end performance at almost every track - but they were mistaken.

Longer engine life per FIM-sealed unit was found at the expense of almost nothing, as developments in components inside the valve train and a new camshaft design radically improved engine reliability, but easing the 'hit' of camshaft on the valves.

The RSV engine maybe even got better in 2014 because it got more rounded and had even more winter development and dyno time than normal.

At the heart of the machine the Aprilia now pumps out 232.5CV at (a probably reduced) 15,000 revs, with a compression ratio of around 15:1.

The cassette gearbox was only a benefit at some times in 2014, with limited ratio options to choose from by regulation and limited opportunities to change them during race weekends. Clutch is an STM unit; exhaust Akrapovic. Airbox, by regulation, is stock.

The 65° vee-four four-stroke engine still bristles with leading edge ancillary tech, including variable height intake trumpets, ride-by-wire throttles as standard and its own electronics package; which is still under the control of Aprilia directly.

The custom APX2 ECU unit is joined by a stock instrumentation cluster from the road machine, which is already configured to show the key elements needed for the riders on track and the

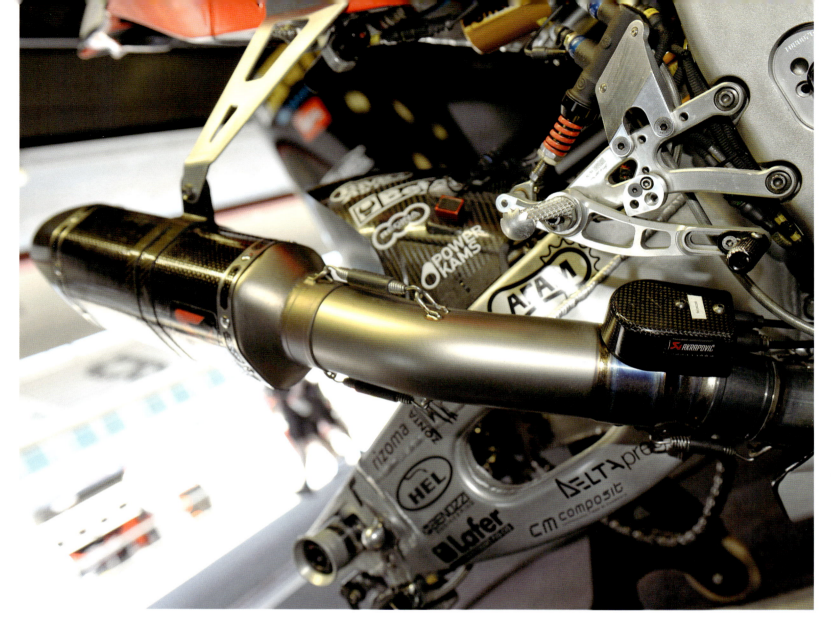

Akrapovic exhaust used a power valve to help control the engine manners on a closed throttle. Swingarm with hole was one of many possible options for this key component

mechanics in the garage.

The twin spar aluminium chassis can run variable head inserts in the steering stem, has an adjustable rear swingarm pivot position and is matched to different rear swingarms depending on the rider preference. No additional headstock bracing for 2014, possibly as the 48mm forks of 2013 disappeared. The older swingarms are more curved and solid looking, but the most recent additions have flatter side elements and bigger holes through their sidewalls to help with stability when the riders start to apply hard throttle exiting turns.

As per regulation, brakes, shocks and other ancillary parts were limited in price and therefore exclusivity, so for brakes the Aprilia used Brembo P4 3034 callipers and a radial pump with reduced free play, and 'T-drive' floating discs, usually 336mm in diameter. The rear was a 218 mm floating disc gripped by a P230 calliper. Thicker 7mm discs were used depending on the track and rider preference.

Front forks and rear shocks were the stock Öhlins units as per the price limitation rules for 2014, of 42mm diameter. No through rod technology, just rod solid piston units. Again, the lap times were hardly hurt by this 'dumbing-down' of available technology.

ENGINE

Type	65° V4 cylinder across the frame, 4-stroke, liquid cooling system, double overhead camshaft (DOHC), four valves per cylinder
Displacement	999 cc
Bore and Stroke	78 x 52.3 mm
Fuelling/Ignition	Variable-height intake ducts controlled by engine control unit, electronic injection with 8 injectors and latest-generation ride-by-wire and inertial input technology
Gearbox	Six-speed cassette gearbox
Maximum Power	232.5CV @ 15,000rpm

CYCLE PARTS

Chassis	Adjustable, aluminium dual beam with pressed and cast sheet elements
Suspension	Öhlins 48mm TRSP25 (through-rod solid piston) forks or TRVSP25 RSP40 Rear (TTX40) (Rod solid piston, 40 mm displacement)
Brakes	Brembo 18 x 18mm master cylinder. 328mm Brembo rotors 'H'-Type discs. Z04 pads
Wheelbase	1,424 mm (variable)
Overall length	2,050 mm
Fuel tank capacity	21 litres fixed
Weight	167 kg

Right above. Öhlins suspension was standard 2014 price-capped kit. Notice hole for exhaust gas sensor next to shock spring collar. Below, exhaust outlets for titanium system. Right below, electronics packed into the nose of the Aprilia racebike

DUCATI
1199 PANIGALE R

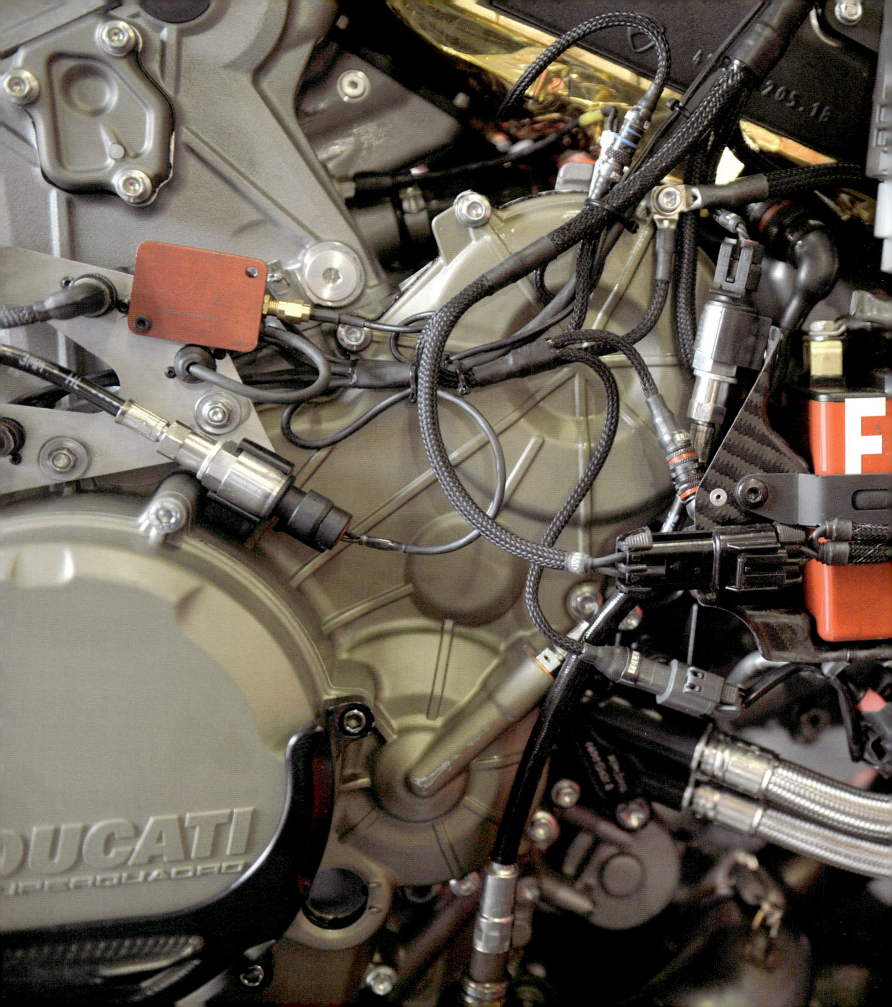

DUCATI
1199 PANIGALE R

BIG RED

IN its second year of SBK existence the 1199R Panigale made the kind of leaps that were expected on track for a company like Ducati, but it was still toiling against the best four-cylinder entries at times. With weight parity, no air intake restrictors, but still with limits on what could be changed inside the vastly oversquare desmodromically timed 90 degree vee-twin engine, the L-shaped motor put out more power than it did in 2013. Maybe ten at the top end.

The watchword in 2014 was 'control' first and foremost, however. Linearity of power production was the key to any kind of success, and with the two hard chargers inside the Ducati family happy to try new things to make the complicated overall design work, progress was slow but sure.

The Panigale chassis, as such, is also the airbox. Forming a monocoque section with the steering stem at one end and the intakes for the EFI system at the other, it was a metallic definition of multi-tasking.

The rear subframe is bolted onto the back of the engine, as is the rear swingarm, with the shock on the left side of the rear cylinder. A funky and asymmetrical bell crank system of rear suspension operation was in place but this time - as per regulation - suspension prices were limited for their Öhlins materials.

The highest allowable prices of €6,500 for a rear shock and €10,000 for a set of forks were the case for all suppliers in the championship.

Weight was an area Ducati worked on with their titanium exhaust and various bolts shaving off a few kilos. A new generator also saved weight but Panigale is still a bit over the 165kg limit for safety in scrutineering post race.

The electronics received a major upgrade at the beginning of the year, and also at mid-season, with MotoGP derived strategies being found inside the existing ECU units from Marelli from around Portimao and America onward. With more processing going on inside the ECU, sitting in front of a false fuel tank section, slots were cut in the side of the 'fake front' of the fuel tank to allow cooling air to get in, but keep the worst of the

DUCATI
1199 PANIGALE R

weather out.

New software strategies were primarily designed to allow more fine-tuning in the areas of anti-wheelie and traction control. Rider changes to the maps on the move were done by a simple array of buttons, one to switch between modes, then up and down buttons to increase of decrease the settings. A full top spec electronic system for the Panigale was reputed to cost around 45,000 Euros, with all sensors and full military-style connectors. Moving the rider around was a key part of the Panigale's tricky chassis set-up cure and Davies had to have padding applied

New electronics strategies arrived mid-season to help the development of a much-improved machine. The unique rear suspension design of the Panigale is as radical now as when it was first seen.

to his fuel tank to keep his weight towards the back for traction.

With their Öhlins shocks and forks limited in price and therefore spec the rear top out damper disappeared from the rear RSP40 rear chocks and the front RSP25 42mm forks were also a step down from 2013. No real change in performance was detected.

In the braking department, Ducati finally made a move to T-type Brembo brakes (around 700 Euros each) after persevering with the round bobbin types long after most others had dropped this technology.

ENGINE

Type	4-stroke L-twin 90°
Displacement	1198 cm3
Bore and Stroke	112 mm x 60.8 mm
Fuelling/Ignition	Electronic injection system, independent motorized elliptical throttle bodies
Gearbox	6 speed, straight cut gears
Maximum Power	>220CV** at 11500rpm at the crankshaft

CYCLE PARTS

Chassis	Aluminium monocoque
Suspension	42 mm pressurized RSP25 upside-down Öhlins fork, single-side aluminium swingarm, with Öhlins RSP40 shock absorber
Brakes	FRONT: Brembo radial P4X30-34 calipers, two Ø 328mm floating discs Optional 336mm) REAR: Radial P2X34 caliper, one 218mm Ø disc
Wheelbase	1450 mm
Overall length	2070 mm
Fuel tank capacity	23.9 litres
Weight	165 kg, with water and oil

The stock streetbike rear swingarm was not unique in being a single sided unit but it was a throwback to the original 916 Ducati that was well known by Ducati engineers.

The astonishingly oversquare vee-twin was a compact but muscular unit when exposed to the world. Not heavily oval shape to the exit of the exhaust from the cylinder head.

EBR
HERO EBR 1190 RX

HOME OF THE BRAVE

IF awards went out for determination, bravery and uniqueness the Hero EBR team would be champions already. It is a miracle of sorts that everyone involved managed to get the required number of homologated machines made to allow the move from AMA racing to WSBK in a very short winter of 2013/2014, but the 1190 RX duly appeared for the first round in its maverick technical set-up.
Unique ideas in production-based bike racing were everywhere.

The rim-mounted front brake was standard to start, but then special rotors and calipers (still cost controlled) arrived as the season went on, with special components from Buell, plus other component suppliers.

The chassis itself on the Buell looks conventional enough in its twin-spar alloy design, until you realise that it is in itself the main fuel tank, of 18 litres. Unable to make this tank any bigger, an ancillary fuel cell of six litres (to the max of 24 allowed in the regulations) was added under the seat. This meant that the battery and electronics then had to be moved, towards the front of the bike.

Chassis and cycle parts design got weirder the closer you looked, with the alloy rear swingarm actually not being a complete hollow twin spar design it looked from outside. The inside 'lid' of the swingarm box-section was mising, just the strengthening webs and gussets of the original swingarm.

Maybe the most unusual aspect of the chassis design, actually a throwback to days gone by, was the semi-laid down - but linkless - rear shock mounting system. On one side of the rear swingarm the rear mounting point was made, with the top of the Öhlins shock bolted directly to the chassis spars. No rising rate link, so no real geometry to play with. Very left field damping values were needed but this aspect of design was seen as a great limit by other teams.

Front forks were from Öhlins, the same 42mm units as everybody else.

The engine in the EBR was a more conventional affair, but at 72° it differed from a 90° Ducati and really needed its balance shaft. Chain driven cams operated four valves per

The chassis as a fuel cell, wrapping over a big bore vee-twin. All the electronics had to go in the nose because of the under seat fuel tank, on a specially made bracket.

ENGINE

Type	ET-V2: 72° V-Twin, liquid Cooled, four-stroke
Displacement	1190cc
Bore and Stroke	106 x 67.5 mm
Fuelling/Ignition	Magneti Marelli Marvel 4.5 with 2 port injectors and 2 showerhead injectors
Gearbox	Gearbox: 6-speed
Maximum Power	over 200bhp

CYCLE PARTS

Chassis	Aluminium frame with integral fuel reservoir and Additional under seat fuel cell
Suspension	Front Suspension: Öhlins FGR300 Rear Suspension: Öhlins TTX36
Brakes	Front Brake: 386mm Single perimeter rotor, 8 piston inside-out calliper Rear Brake: 220mm Disc, 2-piston Hayes Performance Brakes Calliper
Wheelbase	Adjustable
Overall length	2040mm
Fuel tank capacity	23.9 litres
Weight	172kg

cylinder, with a bore and stroke of 106 x 67.5mm making it considerably less oversquare than the Ducati. Reliability was an issue for one rider more than another in the first half of the year, but power was not in the same class as its competitors as the speed trap figures showed at circuits with long straits.

Work was allowed on this machine to a much greater degree than any existing twin cylinder, but the pace of the race calendar mid season, and lack of testing opportunities, stopped any great development until the Laguna round. 8-9 more horsepower was the claim at the end of the season.

Electronics came from the Magneti Marelli Marvel 4.5 ECU and a home-made form of ride-by-wire was adopted, with a visual display of how much the throttle was really open.

The exhaust system in Australia started off as an artisan manufactured one-off system, made in the UK, but as the season went on it was replaced.

EBR
HERO EBR 1190 RX

The single rear shock had no rising rate linkages to play around with, just bolting onto the chassis and swingarm directly.

A more race ready Spark exhaust appeared after the early skirmishes, while the rear swingarm was unchanged from the original all season. Far Right: Unique EBR front braking system.

HONDA
CBR1000RR FIREBLADE

HONDA
CBR1000RR FIREBLADE

NEW OLD SCHOOL

FOR the 2014 season, a new Honda WSBK homologated streetbike. The only issue was that for all the intents and purposes of the rules, all the top line materials added to the SP version of the latest Honda Fireblade streetbike were taken off, and full race parts substituted.

The new engine top end spec on the roadgoing Fireblade was shared with the SP and a claimed 2kw more than before was the starting place for the Ten Kate engine tuners and Cosworth software experts who found both race winning performances and disappointments along the way.

The eight-engine rule was no problems for Honda, even if their engine life went down from 1,900km the year before to 1,500km this year. The adoption of a two-part throttle body, like all the other main screamer bikes in the paddock in 2014, allowed more control and sensitivity in over engine control at the expense of the stress on engines. This was the team's main technical revolution for 2014.

After a serious revamp in 2013, with lots of Honda's MotoGP-inspired software strategies proving too hard to translate to the production derived WSBK championship Fireblade, especially on much more pliable and forgiving tyres, 2014 brought forth another complete change.

It was back to a mix of Cosworth expertise and Ten Kate's own requests, based on the arrival in the team of Italian Massimo Neri – a long respected electronics man in the SBK paddock. Corner-by-corner mapping was possible as the modernity of the CBR's overall electronics system jumped forward.

The sensor package had to change because of the adoption of the split throttle bodies, and also the wiring loom was made differently from before, with an English company creating a new system for 2014.

The rewards when they came were evident, but fleeting, as consistency was the one element still missing from the Honda set-up until nearer the end of the line.

A new design of piston ring also helped with some oil consumption issues that were evident

HONDA
CBR1000RR FIREBLADE

in 2013 on the relatively old-school Honda engine.

The peak power climbed to a claimed 228bhp+.

On the chassis side a change in frame colour was the main chassis alteration but the swingarms were once again highly trick and adjustable, although so settled was the stiffness and geometry that for 2015 the plan was to do without the adjustable sections. As always the shock was buried inside the rear swingarm, in as neat a piece of engineering as could be seen in the whole SBK paddock. A new rear swingarm was rejected after one test in Portimao. Three rear rising rate links, from a vast array of previous possibilities, were also the only options used.

Leon Haslam used a combination of Brembo front brakes and a Nissin rear, while Jonathan Rea continued with the team's official supplier Nissin's front and rear set-up, with Yutaka discs on occasion. The Nissin brake options were 320mm and 330mm in diameter with the Yutaka units coming in at 335mm.

Once again very few changes to the Honda that were visible to the outside world, but once again lots of internal and unseen changes, as Honda continued to try and stay on top of the full Superbike pile, with occasional great success.

ENGINE

Type	Liquid cooled transverse 4-stroke 16-valves DOHC four-cylinder
Displacement	999.8 cm
Bore and Stroke	76 x 55.1 mm
Fuelling/Ignition	Pectel ECU by Cosworth/46mm throttle bodies, Split throttle Ride-By-Wire.
Gearbox	Six speed
Maximum Power	228bhp+

CYCLE PARTS

Chassis	Diamond aluminium composite twin-spar
Suspension	Öhlins 42mm RSP forks, RSP40 rear shock
Brakes	Nissin 320/330mm discs/four pad Nissin callipers, or Yutaka 335mm discs.
Wheelbase	Adjustable
Overall length	2080 mm long
Fuel tank capacity	22.5 litres aluminium
Weight	165 kg

Rea's front end braking set-up was unique in WSB factory terms, with Nissin brake calipers and Yutaka brake discs. Both companies were official team partners, but even so Haslam used Brembo material on his machine.

Above: Unique electronics and display for Honda could truly be customized! Beautifully engineered top yoke. Below: Riders can make software adjustments on the move, via multi-coloured buttons.

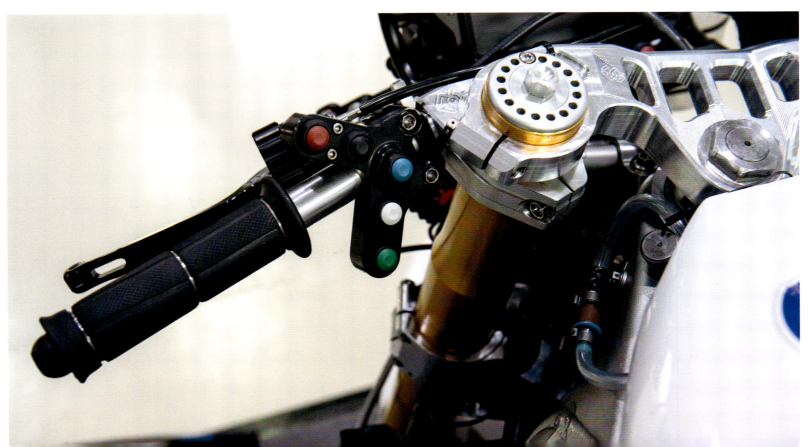

KAWASAKI
NINJA ZX-10R

CHANGES AND SIMILARITIES

FOR Kawasaki the 2013 championship winning bike was an object of loving full factory care and attention again in 2014, with lots of former MotoGP and top level Superbike talents on display in the garages and new parts to try during the winter test sessions. With new rules some things had to change, for engine life and gearbox options to start, and brake and suspension specs at the finish.

The only team in he entire paddock to use Showa suspension, the need for Kawasaki to change their units drastically was negated by this sole supplier status, but the rear shock options changed in 2014, just to deliver the same kind of quality performance as 2013 but in a less expensive package. The 48mm diameter WSBK 'kit' front forks from Showa were much wider than the usual 42mm Öhlins units. One spec of three-way adjustable rear shock, with Showa's twin-tube design, and a 36mm solid piston design, was settled on.

Chassis setting and geometry remained a closely guarded secret, but the front bodywork appeared to have been subtly re-designed in what is effectively a silhouette class, to punch a hole through the air better.

In the engine department internal changes were made for the new limit of eight engines. All in all Kawasaki did not lose any top end compared to 2013, but gained a couple of horsepower, and as a balanced engine package it was as good as anybody else's.

A new engine spec for the mid-season tests had issues that made Kawasaki beat a hasty retreat to the previous spec.

A split throttle body modification continued in 2014, and with close-to GP level electronics and ECU from Magneti Marelli the entire engine management of the Kawasaki was class leading. Slots were evident in the fake front 'fuel tank' panels to let the heat out from the overworked processors inside the ECU.

For the chassis Kawasaki not only continued with their partners Showa but also with

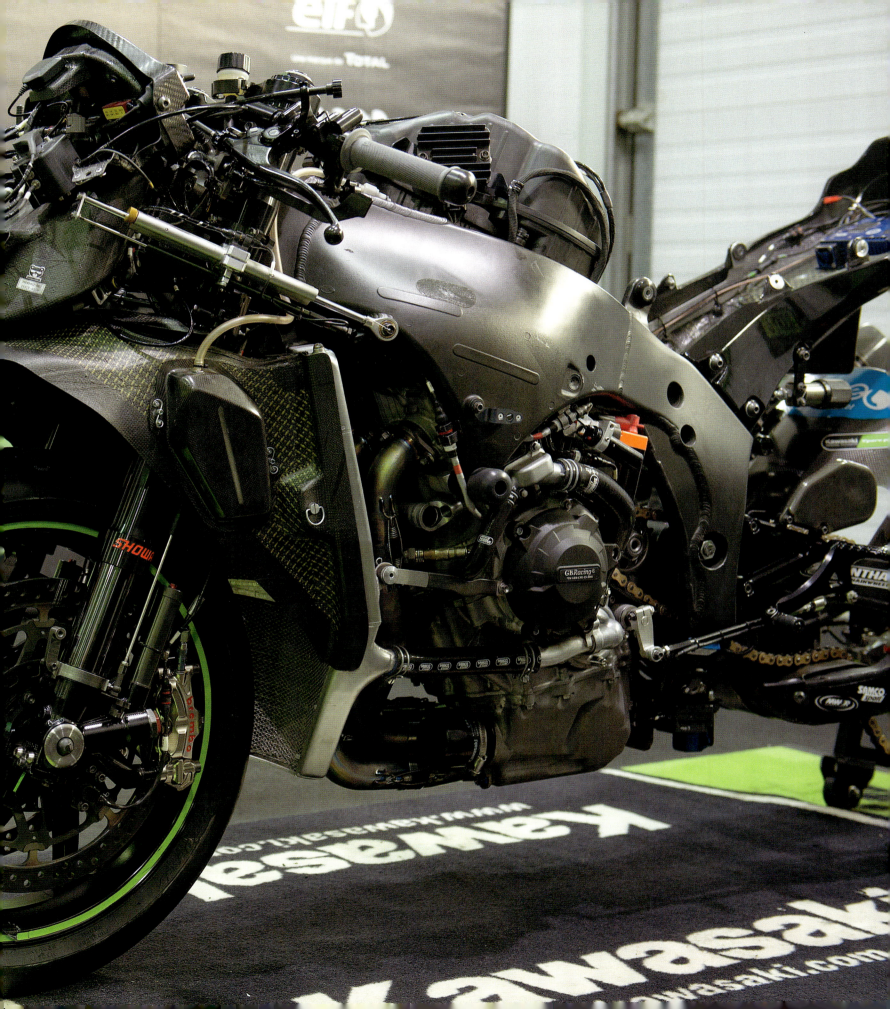

KAWASAKI
NINJA ZX-10R

their unique underslung rear swingarm design with its exposed rear shock absorber laid almost flat.

Easy to change, easy to adjust, it was slightly offset from centre again and ran on a black-painted rear swingarm, with variable rising rate linkages - which were most frequently left alone.

The key to the Kawasaki performance was leaving many aspects alone from race-to-race but on wet settings some advantages found in testing cost a little in outright dry performance afterwards. These had to re-adjusted after the Portimao round.

A new exhaust supplier for 2014, Akrapovic, but there was still a power-valve in the exhaust, with an aerodynamic carbon fibre cover over that area.

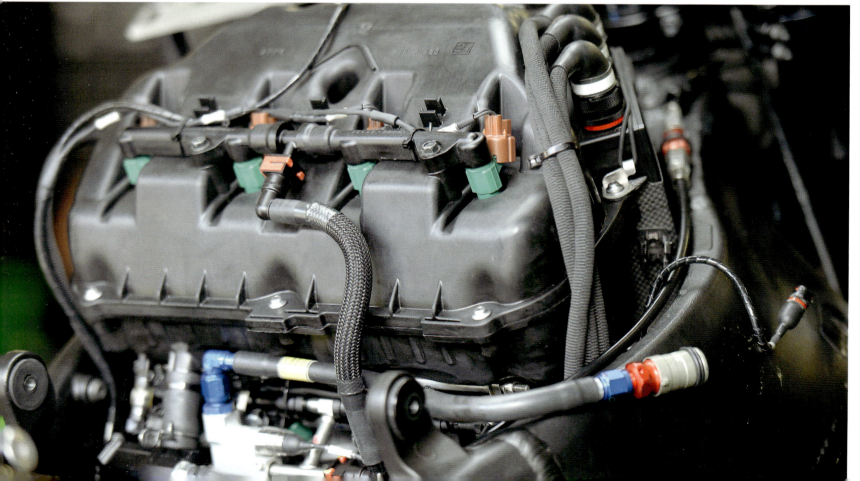

Left above: Unique rear suspension architecture features the rear shock above the underslung swingarm, lying almost horizontally front to back. Left: Stock airbox, and Marelli ECU sits vertically to the nearside of it.

ENGINE

Type	DOHC transverse four-cylinder, four-stroke, liquid cooled
Displacement	999.8 cc
Bore and Stroke	76 x 55 mm
Fuelling/Ignition	Keihin 47mm throttle bodies, Magneti Marelli MHT with Marelli dash and custom software
Gearbox	Six speed
Maximum Power	238bhp+ @ 15,400 rpm

CYCLE PARTS

Chassis	Aluminium twin spar, horizontal back link, progressive
Suspension	Showa WSBK kit forks, 48mm diameter, twin tube 25mm cartridge - rebound, compression and preload. Rear shock Showa T5512 BFR systems, with triple adjusters.
Brakes	Brembo 336mm diameter, H-type disc mounts, aluminium/lithium calipers, Z04 pads. 17 x 18mm master cylinder 34/38mm pistons
Fuel tank capacity	24 litres max
Weight	167kg

As with all other machines that ran Brembos, Sykes and Baz had to use cost-limited materials, but the limit was set neatly at the highest value of the previous best material. Baz and Sykes chose whatever suited their needs race to race but both had made the move to the top level Brembo material the season before in any case.

Top Right: Note gearchange quick shift sensor and wiring. Also, note welding for chassis strengthening which is evident to the top left of the photo. Right: Exhaust design is a key part of engine performance, and carbon fibre saves weight.

SUZUKI
GSX-R 1000

VETERAN PIT BULL

ONCE more into the breach for the British-based Voltcom Crescent Suzuki team as they continued with one of the oldest designs around - and won a race first time out.

The continuation of the GSX-R1000 as a force in SBK 2014 may have been sporadic but it was brilliant on occasions, its nimble chassis nature and some high tech additions meeting on the podium more than once.

The least factory of all the teams in WSBK, they drafted in some new technical talents for 2014. Davide Gentile was the new electronics master, making a great difference to the Motec electronics packages and strategies.

This unique system for one of the top teams was made in Australia but was otherwise looked after by the self-reliant Crescent squad. Engine braking was a constant area of electronic focus. The task was eased by the home-made twin throttle system fitted to the Suzuki this year, with two sets of throttle bodies moved independently of each other to smooth out power delivery and help with back torque limiting. Honda and Kawasaki use similar systems.

The Motec electronic 'hardware' package was simply a kit version, with not quite as much processing power as some, which limited one new area of potential control. Last year a streetbike KTM throttle was the initial input to the ECU system, this year the rider had direct control of two of the throttle butterflies, but the ECU had control of the other two via an electronic actuator. This hybrid system helped the riders in some regards have direct feedback and feel, but it was only there in the first place due to a limit on the ECU system. The response to rider inputs was deemed much faster than with the old system. The engine had some upgrades to bring power up to over 220bhp and the neat two part QD clutch (Crescent's own idea) was retained. With some improvements to the chassis side the Suzuki had the same kind of removable complete tank and seat unit as last year, but both actuation and operation were improved compared to 2014.

Chassis changes were obvious in terms of suspension, with Crescent using the same

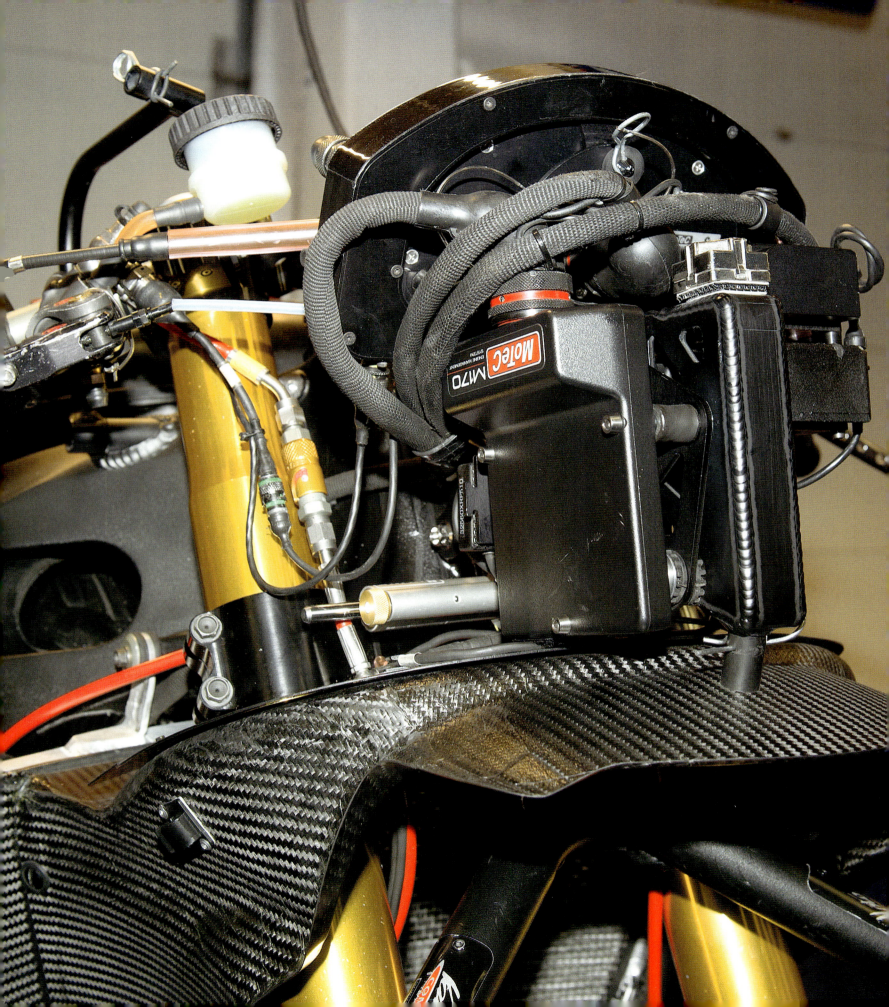

ENGINE

Type	Yoshimura tuned 998.6cc, 4-stroke, 4 cylinder, liquid-cooled, DOHC, 16-valve, TSCC
Displacement	998.6 cc
Bore and Stroke	74.5 x 57.30 mm
Fuelling/Ignition	Motec
Gearbox	6-speed constant mesh
Maximum Power	Over 220bhp @ 14,000

CYCLE PARTS

Chassis	Twin spar aluminium
Suspension	Front suspension: Ohlins FGR200 upside down telescopic forks, 42mm Rear suspension: Ohlins RSP40 single shock
Brakes	Front brakes: Sunstar twin disc 330mm, 4-piston Brembo calliper Rear brake: Sunstar single disc 218mm, 2-piston Brembo calliper
Wheelbase	1440 mm
Fuel tank capacity	23 litres
Weight	165 kg

kind of cost limited Öhlins suspension and Brembo calipers as the others (albeit with Sunstar discs) but things did not stop there.

A new underslung swingarm came on board, adjustable via small grub screws at the start of its life. Laverty was an enthusiastic user and he got a revised one for Laguna. Lowes took more time to get used to it, but moved that way once he had more experience. There were two optional suspension links to start and a third came after the summer break.

With the underslung swingarm there was the possibility of the rear suspension being moved down, which would in turn allow the tank/tail unit to sit lower in the chassis, nearer the centre of gravity. A work in progress.

A bold and still competitive effort, the

Underslung swingarm replaced upwardly curved previous unit. Early versions were adjustable for stiffness via grub screws. Yoshimura tuning and race parts partnership brought forward exquisite exhaust design.

Suzuki now needs to lose more weight to make the next step forward. A titanium Yoshimura 4-1 exhaust was already in use but more weight saving can come with changes to the bodywork and the fuel tank. OZ wheels already cut the rotating mass down.

All-in-all, money and blessings came from Suzuki to allow the team to continue but the 2014 GSX-R was very much a mix of previous Alstare and current Crescent/Yoshimura innovations. A strong - and remarkably race-winning - package.

136

SUZUKI
GSX-R 1000

Above left: Custom array of buttons to adjust software on the move for team's Motec electronics system.
Above right: Entire rear tail unit and fuel cell could be removed as one for ease of maintenance.
Below: Note engine covers to protect against crash damage. Hardly the most modern design of engine or chassis out there, but it was still podium capable.

MV AGUSTA
MV F4 RR

MV AGUSTA
MV F4 RR

NEW TASK FOR OLD MASTER

THE first ever F4, in 750cc guise, came out way back in 1999 but the first real foray into the WSBK world for MV Agusta is the 2014 F4RR.
A project started off in partnership with the Yakhnich Motorsports outfit from Russia, by mid-season they had said their goodbyes and it was stand alone project from MV.

With a full SBK class machine MV had the desirable advantage of having eight engines to use over a season, then they could bring new specifications all season long. Maximum flexibility in the development season of 2014, it was an early aim, but even in Australia at the first round, the F4 would have easily made it as an Evo entry.

Hence the disappointing early results, despite an early 201bhp on tap from the stock engine, even with the catalytic converter fitted. Soon after the start the claim was 225bhp at the crank and the aim by season-end was 235bhp. It may have reached 240, at the crank.

Torque was quoted as 117Nm, driving an EVR clutch.

The engine was able to spin hard from the start, thanks to its quite extreme bore and stroke of 79 x 50.9mm, with titanium valves for the inlet and exhaust already inside even the stock engine. An Arrow exhaust, custom built of course, took care of the outlet side of the engine, but had only two outlets.

Early season the bike weighed in at 170kg plus.

The machine itself was unique in several ways, from its radial valve head design to its tubular steel upper chassis in a four-cylinder format. The two alloy plates that formed the rear swingarm pivot were more conventional on the surface but hid another unique item or two.

The single sided swingarm was a throwback to the original designer Massimo Tamburini's 916, but it gave the bike a unique look in the four cylinder world.

At the beginning this swingarm was a non-race item, albeit on a chassis running custom made Marchesini alloy wheels. Other chassis oddities included the bell crank rear suspension, again like Tamburini designs of old, with an exposed ride height adjuster and a rising rate linkage which pushed the shock from each end as the rear wheel rose.

MV AGUSTA
MV F4 RR

Upside down, in some ways. No fewer than six different rear swingarms were produced in 2014, by the factory itself.

The bank of throttle intakes have variable inlet tract technology already, which made for an even more complicated series of variables for the Magneti Marelli Marvel 4 electronics system to deal with.

A machine with a lot of potential, as the smaller F3 triple has proved in WSS, the F4 is still in its WSBK infancy.

The first changes through the year were to the chassis, with new triple clamps adjusting the offset, different rear suspension links and its specially made wheels.

ENGINE

Type	4-cylinder in line four stroke, 16 valve
Displacement	999.8 cm
Bore and Stroke	79 x 50,9 mm
Fuelling/Ignition	Magneti Marelli Marvel 4
Gearbox	Six-speed
Maximum Power	240 CV at the crankshaft

CYCLE PARTS

Chassis	Tubular trellis, with aluminum alloy rear section
Suspension	Rear Suspension: 36mm Öhlins monoshock Front Suspension: 42mm Öhlins forks
Brakes	Front Brake: Brembo discs 338 mm Ø - Front Caliper Brembo radial 4 pistons with SBS pads Rear Brake: Brembo disc 210 mm Ø Rear Caliper Brembo calipers with SBS pads
Wheelbase	stock 1430 mm
Overall length	Adjustable
Fuel tank capacity	24 litres max
Weight	171 kg

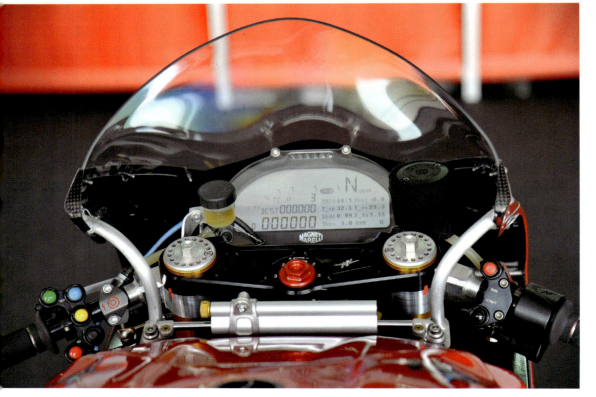

Above: Adjustable footpegs just one example of how no detail is too small to matter for MV Agusta. Left: Magneti Marelli electronics lead to the LCD dashboard. Rider adjustments on the move come via coloured buttons on the left handlebar.

The bell crank style rear suspension is pushed from both ends, the top by a cantilever link operated by a tie rod, the bottom on a link of its own. With a single sided swingarm the rear brake has to travel inboard of the rear wheel, making for a very neat look once the wheel is on.

Spain's David Salom (Kawasaki) was the first rider in history to win the new EVO category title in World Superbike.

EVO CLASS

> *Niccolò Canepa (Ducati) below, and David Salom above, were the best riders in the new EVO class. The Italian and the Spaniard were on top form in this category, and even finished ahead of some factory Superbike riders on occasions. Canepa and Salom often went head to head on the track.*

EVO CLASS

> Above, France's Sylvain Barrier was always quick on the BMW. Below, Australian Bryan Staring (67) and Italian Alessandro Andreozzi (21).

Frenchmen Foret (9) and Guarnoni (11) had an up-and-down season. Scassa (23) was injured for some time while Rizmyer (16) made his debut at the end of the season. Morais (32) had several good races.

TYRES
PIRELLI

TYRES
PIRELLI

IN 2014 Pirelli was confirmed as the Official Tyre Supplier for all classes of the eni FIM Superbike World Championship, having won the tender organized by Dorna, promoter and organiser of the World Championship, in agreement with the FIM, the International Motorcycling Federation. The agreement confirms Pirelli in its current role as sole tyre supplier for all the classes of the FIM Superbike World Championship until the end of the 2018 season.

Over the years, Pirelli has always offered its active contribution to make the competition exciting whilst communicating with all the stakeholders, namely the International Motorcycling Federation, the organiser of the Championship, the teams, riders and the motorcycle manufacturers. Starting from 2004, and now in its eleventh year, the technical partnership established between Pirelli, the teams and riders of the eni FIM Superbike World Championship can now boast the record of the longest running control tyre supplier in the history of motorsports at International level. Established with the primary purpose to reduce the overall cost of running the Championship, the single tyre formula proposed by Pirelli has steadily increased quality and competitiveness, enabling all the riders, teams and motorcycle manufacturers participating to compete for success in the series.

The renewal confirms the leading role in motorsport played by Pirelli and represents a strong continuity with their business strategy. In over a decade of participation as Official Tyre Supplier, the eni FIM Superbike World Championship has enabled Pirelli to develop products which are highly appreciated by the riders and motorcyclists from all over the world and which established themselves as market leaders. Pirelli has been able to achieve this thanks to the ongoing commitment to innovation and development of its products. This work, carried out with the riders of the production derived series, has no equal: in fact, the range of Pirelli racing tyres have travelled a total of more than 1 million kilometres in races with often extreme temperatures. In 2013, keeping true to

TYRES
PIRELLI

the philosophy that has always characterized the commitment and strategy of Pirelli in the FIM Superbike World Championship, that is the use not of prototype tyres but production ones which are sold on the market, Pirelli, for the first time in its history, has abandoned 16.5 inch DIABLO™ Superbike tyres for 17", a size most commonly used by road motorcyclists. The slogan "We sell what we race, We race what we sell" is now a trademark of the brand, proving just how the experience and technology gained in racing should be made available to all motorcyclists. This is also illustrated by the great development work for the race tyres that focus on performance over full race duration, not just for one lap.

Thanks to the dedication that the riders of the Superbike World Championship have placed in testing the new 17-inch tyres since 2014, Pirelli has become the first tyre manufacturer to utilise them in the Endurance World Championship. They are also available to all riders that run in National championships such as the British Superbike Championship, the Italian Championship and German IDM, just to name a few.

Since its 2013 debut the new 17" DIABLO™ Superbike tyres immediately demonstrated excellent performance and in 2014, alongside a new qualifying tyre, has contributed greatly to improving lap times while creating lap records on many circuits in which the Championship has made a stop in the previous years.

2014 was for Pirelli a year especially of great development of its products during the introduction of the new EVO class. During the year the Milanese company has doubled its commitment in terms of design, offering various ad hoc solutions to the EVO category and the Superbike class with the aim of trying to reduce the gap between the two classes. The new EVO class differs from Superbike in terms of horsepower, electronics and engine set-up, providing an opportunity for the fastest riders in this class to be competitive in the races, and consequently, to make the Championship even more balanced and compelling. The data obtained in 2014 relating to the behaviour of the EVO Superbikes, will also be important in respect to 2015 when the grid of the premier class will all run to these specifications.

Important work has been done not only on Superbike slick tyres but also on DIABLO™ Supercorsa, the treaded tyre that is used in the Supersport, Superstock 1000 and 600 classes and in the European Junior Cup series. Again, Pirelli engineers have been working diligently especially at the level of compounds that are now more versatile and efficient.

Finally the tyre manufacturer puts great emphasis in supporting young riders to develop and show their talents in the motorcycling world. This is why over the last three years Pirelli has been supplying tyres to all the riders taking part in the European Junior Cup, the championship which opens the way for the champions of tomorrow.

In the picture below the Pirelli grid girls on the starting grid of the Malaysian round.

> In the above picture the start of Race 1 at Donington Park, bottom left Giorgio Barbier, Pirelli Moto Racing Director, rewards Tom Sykes at the Malaysian round, bottom right the Pirelli team present on track every weekend.

WSS CHAMPIONSHIP

MICHAEL VD MARK | THE CHAMPION

DETERMINED

talented, mature and quick. In just one word: champion. Class of 1992, coming from the town of Gouda in the heart of southern Netherlands, Michael van der Mark succeeded in winning the Supersport World Championship two years after taking the European Superstock 600 title in 2012. No one has ever managed to win both championships before.

Van der Mark grew up within the Ten Kate team and then arrived in production-based racing in 2010, the final round of the European Superstock 600 season as replacement for Frenchman Florian Marino. He was the leading rider for the Ten Kate Junior team in 2011, and finished third overall in the standings that year. The Dutchman was very quick, he won four races but his race management skills were still not honed perfectly. In 2012 he started the season as one of the favourites for the title, but found himself up against Riccardo Russo, with whom he fought for the continental crown right down to the final round at Magny-Cours. With six wins and nine podiums in ten races he was crowned European champion, thus earning his passage into Supersport. Ronald and Gerrit Ten Kate believed a lot in him, they were convinced of the quality of the young Dutchman who however did not let the success go to his head.

Van der Mark comes from a modest family: between races he helps his father as truck driver and during the winter tests he occasionally also drives the team trucks from the Netherlands to Spain. He's a rider from another time with no frills about him, and he always has a smile on his face. He never seems to complain, learns from his own mistakes and at the end of 2013 he finished fourth in the Supersport standings with three podiums to his name. During the summer break he produced a minor miracle: invited by Honda to the Suzuka 8 Hours he won the famous endurance race on his debut. Despite the fact that he had never ridden a Superbike before he proved to be really quick right from first practice, even quicker than experts Jonathan Rea and Leon Haslam. His destiny was written in the stars: the Ten Kate team wanted him in Superbike, but first he had to win the Supersport 600 title.

The start of the season however didn't go as expected: in the sprint race at Phillip Island he crashed out, wasting a golden opportunity. Many observers said that he still

WSS CHAMPION
MICHAEL VD MARK

A very strong braker, Van der Mark matured a lot during the season. Right, celebrations for the title won at Jerez.

had to mature as a rider, but in the second round of the season at Aragon, he went on the rampage: runner-up behind Kenan Sofuoglu, the most successful rider in Supersport history, here he began his climb to the top of the standings. At his home race in the Netherlands the entire crowd was cheering for him. Despite the enormous pressure, van der Mark did not fail to disappoint, and he won the first Supersport race of his career. At Imola he was second, then came wins at Donington Park and Sepang. In Malaysia, the Dutchman proved to be a true champion, edging out the more expert Cluzel in the final stages. At Misano Adriatico he was runner-up behind the Frenchman and then won again at Portimao. At Jerez he had his first chance to win the title and he didn't waste the opportunity. He won the race and the title one month exactly after again winning the Suzuka 8 Hours race in Japan.

Michael van der Mark is a complete champion. Very few riders have his determination on the bike and his charisma in the paddock. He is one of the most-loved riders in the production-based series thanks to his natural character. Well-mannered, always available, he has all the right cards to embark on a successful career and in 2015 he will be going up against the top riders in the championship after being promoted to the factory Honda Superbike team.

Van der Mark on the top of the podium at Jerez. In Spain, the Dutchman won the race and the title, becoming world champion with one round remaining.

WSS CHAMPIONSHIP

Jules Cluzel took his MV Agusta to the top slot three times in 2014, with wins at Phillip Island, Misano and Magny-Cours and eventually finished runner-up in the championship.

21-year-old Florian Marino (above), third overall, had a good season with several podiums and pole position at Assen. Below, Lorenzo Zanetti was again the best Italian rider, and he took a win at his home circuit of Imola.

WSS CHAMPIONSHIP

> Britain's Kev Coghlan (alongside) was always quick on his Yamaha, while the revelation of the year was surely the American rider PJ Jacobsen, making his world championship debut, who picked up a second and a third place.

WSS CHAMPIONSHIP

> Two-time world champion Kenan Sofuoglu had a troubled season, but despite this he took the win at Aragon, while Supersport rookie from Thailand, Ratthapark Wilairot scored a brilliant second place in the night race at Losail.

Veteran Roberto Rolfo (above) managed to take his Kawasaki to a podium spot once, in the rain at Magny-Cours. Irishman Jack Kennedy did the same, taking the runner-up slot at Portimao.

STK1000 FIM CUP

LEANDRO MERCADO | THE CHAMPION

LEANDRO

"Tati" Mercado from Argentina was the winner of the Superstock 1000 FIM Cup after a year full of upsets that only concluded on the final lap of the last round, when Lorenzo Savadori, his closest rival in the championship, crashed with victory in the bag. Mercado never stopped believing he could win the title, never once gave up and in the end he fully deserved the win, which came about not only due to his rival's misfortune.

The races are never finished until the chequered flag is out. It's a golden rule of racing that has existed for ever and it will never be forgotten by Leandro Mercado, the winner of the Superstock 1000 FIM Cup after a chaotic finale at the Magny-Cours circuit in France. The Barni Team rider, called 'Tati' by his younger brother, arrived at the final round of the year determined to take the title. He had five points lead over his rival, Lorenzo Savadori from Italy, but was only eleventh on the grid because he had crashed during Saturday's qualifying session. The Team Pedercini rider instead started from pole position after a good session and with the knowledge that he had a good pace in the wet, conditions in which the race started. Everyone said that Mercado had no chance but the Argentinean made a cautious start in the wet from row 4. Mercado also lost a few positions at the start, but then moved his way back up lap after lap, while Savadori was battling for the win.

On the last lap he was fifth, while Savadori, ahead of him, was virtually on the podium and had the title in his grasp. But a few corners from the flag the

STK1000
THE CHAMPION

> *Mercado didn't have a perfect season but the Argentinean fully deserved his win in the Superstock 1000 FIM Cup.*

Italian put the wheels of his Kawasaki on a tricky part of the track, where a number of riders had crashed out previously, and he did the same. He restarted but it was all futile: the title win went to the Argentinean rider, fourth at the flag ahead of Savadori in sixth.

Class of 1992, Leandro Mercado from the small town of Jesus Maria near Cordoba (Argentina) made his debut in the Superstock 1000 FIM Cup in 2011. In 2012 he immediately moved up into Superbike, and then finished the season in Superstock, where he also raced in 2013, showing that he was ready to fight for the title. In 2014 he was one of the protagonists, together with Savadori. Like the Italian he won two races (at Aragon and Jerez), while Savadori was first at Misano Adriatico and Portimao, and he stepped on the podium twice more (third at Imola and second at Misano Adriatico, while Savadori was second at Aragon and third at Jerez), but unlike the Italian he always scored points. Savadori was in fact forced to retire due to a technical problem at Imola. The fight between the two was a hard-fought one and during the season they were joined by Frenchmen Matthieu Lussiana, winner of the last round at Magny-Cours and on the podium at Assen and Portimao, Romain Lanusse, second in the last race of the year, Czech rider Ondrej Jezek, winner at Imola and second at Assen and Italian Fabio Massei, who scored podium finishes in the two Italian rounds.

2014 was also a good year for South African David McFadden, third at Portimao and often with the frontrunners, but also for Dutchman Kevin Valk, surprise winner at his home round at Assen. The Superstock 1000 FIM Cup was as hard-fought as ever in 2014 and the final outcome demonstrated how difficult this class is.

> *Above, Leandro "Tati" Mercado celebrates his title win. Below from left to right, Augusto Fernandez (European Junior Cup winner), Leandro Mercado and Marco Faccani.*

STK1000
CHAMPIONSHIP

> Above, Lorenzo Savadori (32) was a major protagonist in 2014. Only an error in the final round prevented him from taking the title victory. Below, Frenchman Romain Lanusse.

> Above, Frenchman Matthieu Lussiana, third overall in 2014. Below, South African David McFadden, one of the top riders in this season's Superstock 1000 FIM Cup.

STK600 CHAMPIONSHIP
MARCO FACCANI | THE CHAMPION

MARCO Faccani is twenty years of age, comes from Ravenna, the Adriatic Riviera town in Italy and he is the tenth European Superstock 600 Champion in the category's history. Rookie this year in the entry-level production-based racing category, the Team Italia rider saw off the competition to win the continental title one race before the end, proving to be extraordinarily quick and mature at the same time.

Winning the first race of the year on one's debut, in a category and a championship never seen before, is not an everyday occurrence. If you do that AND win the title as well, then it's obvious that you really have potential. Marco Faccani actually joined the European Superstock 600 Championship as one of the favourites. Despite the fact that he had never taken part before, he was already a well-known face in the Superbike paddock, because in 2013 he raced in the two Italian rounds of the Supersport World Championship as wild-card after doing the domestic series in 2012. Young, reserved but with his head on his shoulders, Faccani lived up to the expectations by winning the first race of the season at Aragon on his debut. The Team Italia man had the task of living up to the previous year's winner, Franco Morbidelli, but he wasn't fazed by this at all. He didn't lose heart either at the next round at Assen, when he had a bad race and only finished tenth in the wet conditions. After the Dutch Round he began a run of positive results that saw him take wins in succession at Imola, Misano Adriatico, Portimao and Jerez, where he took the title with one round left. His only DNF was at Magny-Cours, in the last round of the season, when he was taken out while fighting for the win. With five wins in seven races, four pole positions and three fastest laps to his name, Marco Faccani fully deserved the 2014 European title.

His chief rival on the track was also from the same place: Federico Caricasulo, another

Superstock 600 rookie, began the season with two zeroes to his name. Faccani and Caricasulo put on a spectacular show in every race, even though the classification showed that expert Wayne Tessels was Faccani's true adversary for the title. The Dutchman scored two podium finishes at the start of the season, finishing third at Aragon and Assen, when he took over at the top of the standings, but he then disappointed in the Italian rounds at Imola and Misano Adriatico. In the Portimao race he caused a few problems for Faccani

> *Italian Andrea Tucci, Faccani's team-mate, finished third overall in the European championship in his debut year.*

STK600 CHAMPIONSHIP

Tessels (left) was the true rival for Faccani. Tuuli (below) was quick with the Yamaha, but he didn't score points in three races.

but finished behind in second place, and in the decisive race for the title at Jerez, he was not in the fight for victory. And not even in France, the venue for the final round of the year, when the title had already been clinched, did he manage to win. He actually only finished eleventh, while the real spectacle was provided by the Turkish wild-card Toprak Razgatioglu, who won on his debut in Superstock 600 after setting pole position. Sponsored by the multiple Supersport title winner, his fellow countryman Kenan Sofuoglu, whose number he also has on his bike, Razgatioglu was the second major surprise of 2014. The Superstock 600 FIM European Championship also saw two other interesting young rookies: the Italians Andrea Tucci and Kevin Manfredi. The former took a podium at Aragon, with the runner-up slot behind team-mate Faccani, while the latter finished second at Assen. Both these talented riders were on better form that Belgium's Gauthier Duwelz, the disappointment of 2014, while Finland's Niki Tuuli, winner at Assen and twice more a podium finisher (second at Imola and third at Jerez), had an up and down year.

SUPERBIKE - 2014

Pos	Rider	Nat - Bike	Pts
1°	S. Guintoli	(FR A - Aprilia)	416
2°	T. Sykes	(GBR - Kawasaki)	410
3°	J. Rea	(GBR - Honda)	334
4°	M. Melandri	(ITA - Aprilia)	333
5°	L. Baz	(FRA - Kawasaki)	311
6°	C. Davies	(GBR - Ducati)	215
7°	L. Haslam	(GBR - Honda)	187
8°	D. Giugliano	(ITA - Ducati)	181
9°	T. Elias	(ESP - Aprilia)	171
10°	E. Laverty	(IRL - Suzuki)	161
11°	A. Lowes	(GBR - Suzuki)	139
12°	D. Salom	(ESP - Kawasaki)	103
13°	N. Canepa	(ITA - Ducati)	73
14°	J. Guarnoni	(FRA - Kawasaki)	45
15°	S. Barrier	(FRA - Bmw)	40
16°	L. Camier	(GBR - BMW)	37
17°	C. Corti	(ITA - MV Agusta)	27
18°	S. Morais	(ZA - Kawasaki)	24
19°	A. Andreozzi	(ITA - Kawasaki)	22
20°	F. Foret	(FRA - Kawasaki)	20
21°	L. Lanzi	(ITA - Ducati)	19
22°	B. Staring	(AUS - Kawasaki)	18
23°	M. Neukirchner	(D - Ducati)	17
24°	L. Scassa	(ITA - Kawasaki)	16
25°	G. Rizmayer	(H - Bmw)	7
26°	G. Allerton	(USA - Bmw)	6
27°	K. Bos	(NL - Honda)	5
28°	I. Toth	(H - Bmw)	5
29°	I. Goi	(ITA - Ducati)	5
30°	R. Russo	(ITA - Kawasaki)	5
31°	L. Pegram	(USA - EBR)	2
32°	M. Fabrizio	(ITA - Kawasaki)	2
33°	R. Lanusse	(L - Kawasaki)	1

MANUFACTURERS CHAMPIONSHIP

Pos	Make	Pts
1°	Aprilia	468
2°	Kawasaki	431
3°	Honda	350
4°	Ducati	291
5°	Suzuki	234
6°	BMW	81
7°	MV Agusta	34
8°	EBR	2

SUPERSPORT - 2014

Pos	Rider	Nat - Bike	Pts
1°	M. vd Mark	(NL - Honda)	230
2°	J. Cluzel	(FRA - MV Agusta)	148
3°	F. Marino	(FRA - Kawasaki)	125
4°	L. Zanetti	(ITA - Honda)	112
5°	K. Coghlan	(GBR - Yamaha)	109
6°	P. Jacobsen	(USA - Kawasaki)	99
7°	R. Rolfo	(ITA - Kawasaki)	97
8°	K. Sofuoglu	(TUR - Kawasaki)	94
9°	R. Wilairot	(THA - Honda)	70
10°	R. De Rosa	(ITA - Honda)	70
11°	R. Tamburini	(ITA - Kawasaki)	70
12°	J. Kennedy	(IRL - Honda)	56
13°	M. Bussolotti	(ITA - Honda)	30
14°	A. Nocco	(ITA - Kawasaki)	27
15°	C. Gamarino	(ITA - Kawasaki)	27
16°	K. Wahr	(GER - Yamaha)	26
17°	R. Russo	(ITA - Honda)	25
18°	F. Menghi	(ITA - Yamaha)	20
19°	V. Leonov	(RU - Honda)	19
20°	M. Roccoli	(ITA - MV Agusta)	15
21°	D. Schmitter	(SUI - Yamaha)	14
22°	L. Mahias	(FRA - Yamaha)	13
23°	G. Gowland	(GBR - Triumph)	9
24°	Z. Zaidi	(MAL - Honda)	7
25°	T. Coveña	(NL - Kawasaki)	7
26°	L. Marconi	(ITA - Honda)	5
27°	M. Law	(GBR - Kawasaki)	5
28°	V. Debise	(FRA - Honda)	4
29°	M. Davies	(AUS - Honda)	3
30°	N. Calero	(ESP - Honda)	3
31°	F. Rogers	(GBR - Honda)	1

MANUFACTURERS CHAMPIONSHIP

Pos	Make	Pts
1°	Honda	251
2°	Kawasaki	181
3°	MV Agusta	162
4°	Yamaha	121
5°	Triumph	9

SUPERSTOCK 1000 - 2014

Pos	Rider	Nat - Bike	Pts
1°	L. Mercado	(AR - Ducati)	117
2°	L. Savadori	(ITA - Kawasaki)	109
3°	M. Lussiana	(FRA - Kawasaki)	84
4°	R. Lanusse	(FRA - Kawasaki)	73
5°	D. McFadden	(ZA - Kawasaki)	70
6°	O. Jezek	(CZE - Ducati)	69
7°	F. Massei	(ITA - Ducati)	67
8°	K. Smith	(GBR - Honda)	55
9°	K. Valk	(NL - Kawasaki)	52
10°	F. D'Annunzio	(ITA - BMW)	45
11°	J. Day	(USA - Honda)	42
12°	B. Nemeth	(HUN - Kawasaki)	28
13°	R. Muresan	(RO - BMW)	21
14°	S. Suchet	(CH - Kawasaki)	18
15°	J. Metcher	(AUS - Ducati)	16
16°	F. Sandi	(ITA - BMW)	16
17°	C. Bergman	(SWE - Kawasaki)	13
18°	S. Egea	(FRA - Kawasaki)	11
19°	S. Grotzkyj G.	(ITA - Kawasaki)	10
20°	R. Pagaud	(FRA - Kawasaki)	10
21°	J. Alviz	(ESP - Kawasaki)	9
22°	A. Alarcos	(ESP - Kawasaki)	8
23°	A. Schacht	(DNK - Ducati)	8
24°	R. Castellarin	(ITA - BMW)	7
25°	N. Walraven	(NL - Suzuki)	6
26°	J. Ayer	(CH - Kawasaki)	5
27°	K. Calia	(ITA - Aprilia)	4
28°	M. Moser	(DEU - Ducati)	4
29°	A. Maurin	(FRA - Kawasaki)	2
30°	A. Butti	(ITA - Kawasaki)	1

MANUFACTURERS CHAMPIONSHIP

Pos	Make	Pts
1°	Kawasaki	149
2°	Ducati	141
3°	Honda	71
4°	BMW	57
5°	Suzuki	6
6°	Aprilia	4

STANDINGS & CHAMPIONS

SUPERSTOCK 600 - 2014

1°	M. Faccani	(ITA - Kawasaki)	131
2°	W. Tessels	(NL - Suzuki)	88
3°	A. Tucci	(ITA - Kawasaki)	78
4°	N. Tuuli	(FI - Yamaha)	74
5°	F. Caricasulo	(ITA - Honda)	66
6°	I. Mikhalchik	(UKR - Kawasaki)	61
7°	G. Duwelz	(BE - Yamaha)	48
8°	L. Salvadori	(ITA - Kawasaki)	46
9°	K. Manfredi	(ITA - Honda)	38
10°	E. Lahti	(FI - Yamaha)	32
11°	M. Rinaldi	(ITA - Yamaha)	29
12°	S. Casalotti	(ITA - Yamaha)	27
13°	T. Razgatioglu	(TUR - Kawasaki)	25
14°	R. Bodis	(HUN - Honda)	23
15°	M. Marchal	(FRA - Yamaha)	22
16°	A. Dumont	(FRA - Yamaha)	20
17°	A. Nestorovic	(AUS - Yamaha)	19
18°	J. Puffe	(GER - Kawasaki)	18
19°	D. Stirpe	(ITA - Kawasaki)	16
20°	A. Zaccone	(ITA - Honda)	16
21°	R. Hartog	(NL - Suzuki)	13
22°	H. Clere	(FRA - Yamaha)	11
23°	G. Sabatino	(ITA - Yamaha)	11
24°	N. Morrentino	(ITA - Yamaha)	10
25°	C. Rouse	(GBR - Honda)	9
26°	R. Caruso	(ITA - Kawasaki)	7
27°	A. Pittet	(CH - Yamaha)	7
28°	T. Baken	(BE - Yamaha)	6
29°	R. Mercandelli	(ITA - Yamaha)	5
30°	C. Gobbi	(ITA - Yamaha)	5
31°	J. Lewis	(AUS - Honda)	5
32°	K. Zeelen	(NL - Kawasaki)	5
33°	M. Canducci	(ITA - Honda)	3
34°	F. Monti	(ITA - Honda)	2
35°	M. Berchet	(FRA - Yamaha)	1
36°	V. Lagonigro	(ITA - Yamaha)	1
37°	G. De Gruttola	(ITA - Kawasaki)	1
38°	V. Patronen	(FI - Yamaha)	1

WORLD SUPERBIKE

1988	F. MERKEL	USA	HONDA
1989	F. MERKEL	USA	HONDA
1990	R. ROCHE	F	DUCATI
1991	D. POLEN	USA	DUCATI
1992	D. POLEN	USA	DUCATI
1993	S. RUSSELL	USA	KAWASAKI
1994	C. FOGARTY	GBR	DUCATI
1995	C. FOGARTY	GBR	DUCATI
1996	T. CORSER	AUS	DUCATI
1997	J. KOCINSKI	USA	HONDA
1998	C. FOGARTY	GBR	DUCATI
1999	C. FOGARTY	GBR	DUCATI
2000	C. EDWARDS	USA	HONDA
2001	T. BAYLISS	AUS	DUCATI
2002	C. EDWARDS	USA	HONDA
2003	N. HODGSON	GBR	DUCATI
2004	J. TOSELAND	GBR	DUCATI
2005	T. CORSER	AUS	SUZUKI
2006	T. BAYLISS	AUS	DUCATI
2007	J. TOSELAND	GBR	HONDA
2008	T. BAYLISS	AUS	DUCATI
2009	B. SPIES	USA	YAMAHA
2010	M. BIAGGI	ITA	APRILIA
2011	C. CHECA	ESP	DUCATI
2012	M. BIAGGI	ITA	APRILIA
2013	T. SYKES	GBR	KAWASAKI
2014	S. GUINTOLI	FRA	APRILIA

FIM SUPERSTOCK 1000

Year	Rider	Country	Bike
2005	D. VAN KEYMEULEN	BEL	YAMAHA
2006	A. POLITA	ITA	SUZUKI
2007	N. CANEPA	ITA	DUCATI
2008	B. ROBERTS	AUS	DUCATI
2009	X. SIMEON	BEL	DUCATI
2010	A. BADOVINI	ITA	BMW
2011	D. GIUGLIANO	ITA	DUCATI
2012	S. BARRIER	FRA	BMW
2013	S. BARRIER	FRA	BMW
2014	L. MERCADO	AR	DUCATI

WORLD SUPERSPORT

1999	S. CHAMBON	FRA	SUZUKI
2000	J. TEUCHERT	GER	YAMAHA
2001	A. PITT	AUS	KAWASAKI
2002	F. FORET	FRA	HONDA
2003	C. VERMEULEN	AUS	HONDA
2004	K. MUGGERIDGE	AUS	HONDA
2005	S. CHARPENTIER	FRA	HONDA
2006	S. CHARPENTIER	FRA	HONDA
2007	K.. SOFUOGLU	TUR	HONDA
2008	A. PITT	AUS	HONDA
2009	C. CRUTCHLOW	GBR	YAMAHA
2010	K. SOFUOGLU	TUR	HONDA
2011	C. DAVIES	GBR	YAMAHA
2012	K. SOFUOGLU	TUR	KAWASAKI
2013	S. LOWES	GBR	YAMAHA
2014	M. VD MARK	NL	HONDA

SUPERSPORT WORLD SERIES

1997	P. CASOLI	ITA	DUCATI
1998	F. PIROVANO	ITA	SUZUKI

EUROPEAN SUPERSTOCK 1000

2000	J. ELLISON	GBR	YAMAHA
2001	J. ELLISON	GBR	SUZUKI
2002	V. IANNUZZO	ITA	SUZUKI
2003	M. FABRIZIO	ITA	SUZUKI
2004	L. ALFONSI	ITA	YAMAHA

EUROPEAN SUPERSTOCK 600

Year	Rider	Country	Bike
2005	C. CORTI	ITA	YAMAHA
2006	X. SIMEON	BEL	SUZUKI
2007	M. BERGER	FRA	YAMAHA
2008	L. BAZ	FRA	YAMAHA
2009	G. REA	GBR	HONDA
2010	J. GUARNONI	FRA	YAMAHA
2011	J. METCHER	AUS	YAMAHA
2012	M. Vd MARK	NED	HONDA
2013	F. MORBIDELLI	ITA	KAWASAKI
2014	M. FACCANI	ITA	KAWASAKI

Printed by
D'Auria Printing SPA - Ascoli Piceno
November 2014